All Time Be
Thinking

G000075387

2 Manuscripts In A Book With
Loads Of Logic Games And
Riddles For Adults

Karen J. Bun

This book consists of:

1. 101 Lateral Thinking Puzzles: The Best Logic Games And Riddles Book For Seniors And Adults

2. 61 Lateral Thinking Puzzles: The Entry Level Logic And Riddle Book Designed For Family After-Dinner Activities

101 Lateral Thinking Puzzles

The Best Logic Games and Riddle Book for Seniors and Adults

Karen J. Bun

Bluesource And Friends

This book is brought to you by Bluesource And Friends, a happy book publishing company.

Our motto is **"Happiness Within Pages"**
We promise to deliver amazing value to readers with our books.
We also appreciate honest book reviews from our readers.

Connect with us on our Facebook page
www.facebook.com/bluesourceandfriends and stay tuned to our latest book promotions and free giveaways.

Don't forget to claim your FREE books!

Brain Teasers:
https://tinyurl.com/karenbrainteasers
Harry Potter Trivia:
https://tinyurl.com/wizardworldtrivia
Sherlock Puzzle Book (Volume 2)
https://tinyurl.com/Sherlockpuzzlebook2

Also check out our other books

"Rookstorm Online Saga"
https://tinyurl.com/rookstorm

"Korman's Prayer"
https://tinyurl.com/kormanprayer

"The Convergence"
https://tinyurl.com/bloodcavefiction

"The Hardest Sudokos In Existence (Ranked
As The Hardest Sudoku Collection Available In
The Western World)"
https://tinyurl.com/MasakiSudoku

Introduction

First, I would like to thank you for choosing *101 Lateral Thinking Puzzles*. This book is here to provide you with 101 puzzles that will work your brain in ways you've never worked it before. These puzzles are a great way to pass time.

The difficulty level of these puzzles varies, but no matter how difficult you may find them to be, there is always an answer. Even if you answer the puzzle incorrectly, you may find it fun to explain why your answer could be correct as well.

These are also great to use for a game night with friends and family. Quiz them to see how much they know. You never know what kind of answers you may get. All of these puzzles are lateral thinking puzzles—meaning you won't need a calculator nor pen and paper. All you need is your brain. The puzzles may be short or long, but they give you just enough information to figure out the answer. Make sure you don't over analyze them; otherwise, you may end up missing the answer all together.

The puzzles are straight through from one to 101, and the answers follow in the next chapter. The puzzles and answers are clearly numbered, and each has a title so that you don't have to guess whether you are looking at the right one or not. Above all else, have fun while solving the puzzles.

Puzzles

1. He Lives on the 12th Floor

There is a man who lives on the 12th floor of an apartment building. Each morning, he rides the elevator down to the lobby and leaves for work. When he returns home from work, he gets in the elevator, and, if somebody else was in the elevator or if it rained that day, he would travel straight up to his floor. Else, he would ride it to the 10th floor, and then walk up two flights of stairs to get to his apartment. Why?

2. Burning Fire

Jonathan wakes up on an island that is covered in trees. A strong wind starts blowing from the West. Then, the west end of the island is struck by lightning, and causes the forest to catch fire. It's a horrible fire—nothing will stop it, and the fire was going to burn away the entire island and kill Jonathan as well. The island is surrounded by cliffs, so he is unable to jump off. He doesn't have any means to put out the fire either. What can Jonathan do in order to survive the fire?

3. A Recorded Murder

A man has been discovered dead, and it appeared to be a suicide. When the police arrive, they find him with a tape recorder in one hand and a gun in the other. As the police are investigating the crime scene, they step over to the cassette recorder and press play. The tape plays, and they can hear the man say, "I have nothing else to live for. I can't go on," then there is a gunshot. After they have listened to the tape, they realize that it was actually a homicide and not a suicide. How did they figure this out?

4. A Locked Storeroom

There is a storeroom in your home that you keep locked with a padlock that doesn't need a key to close it, but needs one to open it. You have the only key to the padlock. You decide to take some of your old stuff into your storeroom. After moving everything in carefully, you lock it up. The following day, you find somebody dead in the storeroom.

You live by yourself and have the only key, so the police believe that you are the murderer. You can't figure out how this could happen until you think of something. It is possible that somebody could get a body into your storeroom.

Can you figure out how, so that you can clear your name?

5. A Coin in a Glass Bottle

A guy shows you a trick. He places a coin inside of a glass bottle. He closes the bottle by placing a cork at the top. Now, he takes the coin out of the bottle without removing the cork or breaking the bottle. How did he do this?

6. The Wish of a Servant

In a village, there once was a master and his servant. After about 30 years of service, the master becomes very ill and is going to die. One day, the master calls in his servant and tells him he is going to grant him one wish. It can be anything—but only one wish. He gives him a day to think about what he wants. The servant is happy about this and goes to talk to his mother. His mother is blind and asks her son to wish for her eye-sight restored. Then he talks to his wife. She is excited, and asks him to wish for them to have a son. Then he talks to his father, who has wanted to be rich for a long time, so he asks him to wish for money.

The following day, the servant makes one wish that fulfils all of his family's wishes. What was the wish?

7. 100 Coins

You are in a dark room that has 100 coins all over the floor. Ten are facing heads-up and 90 are facing tails-up. You aren't able to feel or see anything to figure out which side of the coin is facing up. How can you divide the coins between two piles so that both have the same number of heads-up coins?

8. A Sunday Morning Murder

One Sunday morning, a woman gets up to find that her husband isn't in bed. She walks to his study, knowing that he often gets up early to work on things. She discovered that he is dead, and quickly calls the police. When the police arrive, they call the wife and the staff in to speak with all of them. They ask what they were doing during the time of the murder. The wife tells them that she was still asleep at that time. The butler said that he was cleaning out the closet. The gardener tells them that he was picking vegetables. The maid tells them that she was getting the mail. The cook tells them that he was fixing breakfast.
The police are able to immediately arrest the murderer. Who is the murderer, and how do you know?

9. A Romantic Trip

Mr. and Mrs. Walbush took a trip into the mountains. Two days later, Mr. Walbush comes home alone and goes to the police, telling them that Mrs. Walbush had fallen to her death.
The following day, Detective Rayburn visits Mr. Walbush and arrests him for murdering his wife. Walbush confesses his guilt and asks the detective how he figured that he was the killer.
Rayburn explained that he contacted a travel agent and asked for a little information.
What did the travel agent tell the detective?

10. The Man in the Baggy Suit

At the end of Baker Street, there has been a gruesome murder. The police's main suspect is a man name Theodore Williams.

One of the witnesses said that the man had been traveling across the park when they saw another person being shot in the stomach. They said he had blonde hair, brown eyes, and was wearing a baggy suit, which fit Theodore Williams to a T. Theodore is asked to for his side of the story, "Well," Theodore began, "I was in the park when I saw this guy walking. Suddenly, some guy ran up behind him and shot him. I quickly ran home." The police then asked Theodore to describe the man. He said, "He had a brown hair, brown mustache, and was wearing a baggy suit."

One of the officers turned to the others and said, "I do believe he is lying." How was he able to figure this out?

11. The Cottage Life

There is a wealthy man who lives alone in a small cottage located off the main road. Since he is partially handicapped, everything he needed was always delivered to his home. One Thursday, the mailman was bringing his mail and saw that the door was open. Peeking through it, he saw the man lying in blood. The mailman immediately called the police. Once the police officers arrived, they looked over the things at the crime scene. On the porch, they noticed that there were two bottles of spoiled milk, Monday's paper, unopened mail, and a catalog. The police believe that he has been murdered, and is certain that they have figured out who did it. Who do they believe is their number one suspect?

12. Came Up a Little Short

A man calls up his daughter and asks her to buy him some things he needs for his trip. He tells her that she can find enough money for the items in an envelope on his desk. She sees the envelope with "98" written on the outside.

She purchases $90 worth of things, but when she has to pay for it, she not only didn't get $8 back, but she was short on cash. How much was she short by, and why?

13. The Bamboo Pole

Dr. Rage was spending time with Scott, his cousin, in Scott's lakeside cabin. He was helping Scott create his will. Since Rage was Scott's only living relative, most of Scott's estate was going to him. One day, Scott ran to Dr. Rage, very upset. "Doctor," he started, "I have received a message that a man named George plans on hurting me. He is going to be here really soon. Where should I go? I have no place to hide. If he discovers where I am, he is going to end up killing me. I can't flee farther into the woods; I don't have the time."

Dr. Rage took a moment to think, and then got a five foot long bamboo pole that had a diameter that matched a quarter. "Scott, let's go to the lake. The lake is only four feet deep. You can lay on the bottom and use the pole to breathe; George won't be able to find you. I'll stay in the brush with a gun, and I'll kill him if he comes here. Once he is gone, I will swim into the lake to get you."

Scott agrees to the plan and lies down in the lake, using the pole to breathe. After some time, a ranger comes by. He discovers Scott's dead body in the lake. Dr. Rage let the police know of what had happened—that Scott probably ended up panicking and died. The police arrest Dr. Rage for murdering Scott. Why?

14. Three Switches, One Bulb

You can see three light switches on the outside wall of a room. One controls the light inside. With the door is closed, you are allowed to flip the switches as much as you want.

You can go inside—only once though—to see the light. The light can't be seen while outside, and the switches can't be flipped while inside.

Nobody else is there to help you, and the room doesn't have any windows. Based on this information, how can you figure out which of the switches controls the light?

15. Poisoned Juice

You have 1,000 bottles of juice, and one of which is poisoned. The poison causes the juice to taste bitter. You also have the antidote to the poison. You want to figure out which juice contains the poison. What is the smallest number of sips that you have to take in order to figure this out?

16. Hotel Room

A woman is in her hotel room, when there is a knock on the door. She opens the door to find a man that she does not know. He says, "I'm sorry, I think I made a mistake. I thought this was my room." He takes off down the hall and gets into the elevator. The woman quickly phones security.

What made the woman suspicious?

17. A Mysterious Death

Bill and Shane are two popular politicians. They decide to meet up in a club to discuss how they can work to overthrow their party's leader. They both order vodka on the rocks. As soon as Shane's drink is sat on the table, he downs it and orders a second one. When the second one comes to the table, he drinks it down in one gulp, but waits to order a third. Meanwhile, Bill has been sipping on his first glass of vodka. He suddenly collapses on the table, dead. Both men were supposed to be assassinated. Why did Shane live, but Bill die?

18. A Kidnapped Child

There once was a rich man, whose son was kidnapped. The kidnappers left a ransom note that told the man to take a valuable diamond to a telephone booth in the middle of a public park. The rich man informed the police of this. The police sent out some plainclothes officers and surrounded the park, so that they could follow the criminal or the messenger. The rich man arrived at the telephone booth when he was supposed to, and followed all of the instructions, but the police found that they were completely powerless to prevent the diamond from leaving the park and reaching the villain. What did the villain do to ensure that he didn't get caught?

19. The Poisoned Apple

Samantha Gills invited a possible victim over for lunch. They feasted on a hearty meal of roast duck with a wide selection of fresh veggies, and they washed it all down with the finest French wine.

After they had finished their meal with some freshly picked figs and grapes, Samantha said, "There is only one apple left. I insist that you have it." "No," her guest said, "I couldn't." "Tell you what, we are going to share it," Samantha stated.

She promptly sliced the apple into two neat halves with her sharpest knife. Samantha and her guest enjoyed their apple halves, and then suddenly, the guest's eyes rolled back in her head and she keeled over, stone-cold dead.

Why was the victim poisoned, but Samantha was fine when they ate the same apple?

20. Three Rosebushes

A long time ago, there was an evil wizard. He kidnapped three women from their homes and transformed them into three rosebushes that looked exactly alike. He planted them all in his garden. One of the women that he kidnapped had a husband and child, and they begged the wizard to allow her to see them.

He agreed. At night, he would take the woman to her house. Then, the next morning, he would take her back to his home. The following day, the husband decided that he would try to rescue her. He snuck into the garden of the wizard. He looked at the three identical rosebushes to try and figure out which one could possibly be his wife. Suddenly, he realized which one of the rosebushes was his wife, and took her back home with him. How did he know which one of the rosebushes was his wife?

21. A Dead Boyfriend

It was a man's birthday, and his girlfriend was planning him a surprise birthday party. When she went to his house, she found him dead. Beside him was a note that read, "Happy Birthday, Friend." She phoned the police, and as they investigated, they found that the victim's girlfriend had an ex-boyfriend, and they suspected him. They, unfortunately, didn't have any obvious evidence that he was to blame. While they searched through the suspect's car, the police noticed the girlfriend's address written on an envelope. They thought that they might be able to check out the handwriting to match the two. The scientist in charge of this came to work early the next morning. It was 7 am. Glancing out the window, he stared at the rising sun. He then realized how he could prove that the ex-boyfriend was the killer. How was he able to do this?

22. The Logical Cannibals

A reckless explorer wanders into a village and gets himself captured by logic-loving cannibals. He was taken before the chief and told, "You are now allowed to speak your last words. If what you say is false, we will kill you slowly. If your statement is true, we will kill you quickly."
The man took a moment to think, and then he made his statement. Perplexed, the cannibals realized that they can't do

anything else but to let him go. What were the explorer's last words?

23. The Six Grave Plots

One day, you are wandering through a cemetery, and see a mark that is in front of a six-plot grave. You read its inscription: Here lie…
2 Grandmothers with their 2 Granddaughters
2 Husbands with their 2 Wives
2 Fathers with their 2 Daughters
2 Mothers with their 2 Sons
2 Maidens with their 2 Mothers
2 Sisters with their 2 Brothers
There are only six corpses buried here and all of them were born legitimately. There is no incest in the family line. How can this be possible?

24. The Traveling Monk

One morning, at exactly 7 am, a monk starts his journey up the side of a very steep mountain to visit a temple. The trail is very winding and narrow, but it is the only way to get there. As he is climbing, he walks at different speeds, and will sometimes stop to eat and rest, but stays on the path and doesn't go backwards. At precisely 7 pm, the monk makes it to the temple and stays the night.
The next morning, at exactly 7 am, the monk leaves and starts walking back down. He walks back down the same path. Again, he walks at varying speeds, stopping from time to time to drink and eat, but he doesn't ever step off of the path, and he never travels backwards. 12 hours later, by 7 pm, the monk makes it back to the bottom.
During both trips, is there a place the monk would occupy at the same time? How do you know this?

25. Her Lazy Daughter

There is a wealthy wise old woman who is afraid that her daughter is lazy, and because of this, believes that she is stupid. The old woman had stipulated in her will that, once she passes away, all of her assets should be liquidated, and that check be written for the complete amount.

The check was then to be placed inside one of three envelopes. The other two envelopes should be filled with blank paper. If the daughter was able to figure out from the statements in each of the envelopes which one contained the check, then should would inherit all of her mother's fortune. Otherwise, the money would be sent to one of the woman's favorite animal charities.

The daughter shouldn't touch any of the envelopes. She had to make her decisions based solely on the statements on the envelopes. The daughter was told that only one of the statements on the envelopes was true, and that the other two statements were false.

The statements on the envelopes are:

This envelope does not have the check.

This envelope has the check.

The second envelope does not have the check.

Which one of the envelopes should the daughter choose?

26. An Ancient Temple Mystery

There was once a shrine in India that used to house three idols that were identical, and spoke to respective devotees.

These idols represented the God of Truth, the God of Falsehood, and the God of Diplomacy.

The pilgrims would travel from all around the world to have these gods answer their deepest questions, but there was a slight problem: Since a person could not tell the idols apart, the devotees were unsure as to which idol they needed to talk to, and they didn't know if they should believe what the god said. One day, a man asks, "Which god is in the center?" to every one of the idols. The one located to the left said it was the God of Truth. The one in the center said it was the God of Diplomacy. The one of the right said it was the God of Falsehood. The man then told everybody that he had solved the mystery.

27. A Servant Has Gone Missing

There is a King who has 100 identical servants. Each of the servants is ranked from one to 100. Before bed, they all come in randomly, and tells the King their rank, and to let him know that he has finished his work for the day.

The King's aide tells him one day, that one of the servants is missing and they don't know which one.

Before the start of the check-ins, the King gets a piece of paper so that he can figure out which one of the servants has gone missing. Unfortunately, all that the aide can find is a small piece of paper that only one number can be written on at a time. The King can erase the number and write a new number down all he wants, but only one number can be on there.

The King can't remember things, and he won't be able to remember every single number that the servants say as they report in, so the paper has to help him.

How can the paper be used to help him figure out who is the missing servant?

28. The Murder of His Ex-Wife

"Who shot her?" screamed Mark as he ran into the hospital only three minutes after his ex-wife had been declared dead from a gunshot wound through her head.

"I will be with you in just a minute, Sir," said Detective Higgins. "We need to ask you a few routine questions: The two of you have been divorced for six months, but you still live in the same house, is that right?"

"That's right."

"Have you two had any troubles recently?"

"Well, yesterday, when I said I had to go away on a business trip, she threatened to kill herself. In fact, I had to grab a bottle of iodine out of her hand that she was about to drink. When I left yesterday evening at seven, however, and told her that I was spending the night with a friend, she didn't make any objection. When I came back into town this afternoon, I called home, and the maid answered."

"What did the maid tell you?"

"She said, 'Mark, they took the poor mistress to St. Peter's Hospital about half an hour ago. Please hurry after her.' She was crying hysterically, so I wasn't able to get anything else out of her. I hurried here. Where is she?"

"The nurse will show you."

"This is a very odd case," said Inspector Felix, "These modern type people are just too much for me. A man and woman living together after getting a divorce..."

"An odd case, indeed it is. You better go after him and detain him. If he didn't kill her, himself, I'm sure he knows exactly who did."

Why does the detective believe that Mark killed his wife?

29. Mislabeled Boxes

In front of you are three boxes. In one of the boxes, there are red marbles. In another box, there are blue marbles. In the last box, there is a mixture of red and blue marbles. All of the labels on the boxes have been mixed up, so that none of the boxes are correctly labeled.

You have to re-label the boxes so that they are correct. Of course, you could peek into each of the boxes to see what is inside, but can it be done without looking in each of the boxes? How can you reach inside one of the boxes, pull out a marble, and re-label the boxes correctly?

30. The Five Suspects

You are the detective on the scene of a heinous crime. There are five suspects – one of whom is the killer. Your job is to interrogate the suspects. Each of them will give you one statement. You find out later that only three of the statements are true.

Their statements are:

Ralph: Steven committed the murder.

Jackie: I did not do it.

Barrett: It was not Stacey.

Steven: Ralph is lying when he says I did it.

Stacey: Jackie is telling the truth.

Which one of the suspects is the murderer?

31. Their Five Jealous Husbands

A major flood has swept through the town, and five married couples are surrounded by water and need to escape from their position in a boat that is only able to hold three people at a time. Every one of their husbands is so jealous that the he won't let his wife be on the boat or on either bank with another man unless he is present.

What is the quickest way that the five couples can get across from the flood? You can call the men A, B, C, D, and The, and the women 1, 2, 3, 4, and 5. Going across and back counts as two crossings and they can't use any tricks like swimming or using ropes.

32. His 17 Horses

There is a farmer who has 17 horses, and wants to divide them between his three boys. The farmer stated that the eldest gets half, the middle gets a third, and the youngest gets a ninth. After the farmer died, they couldn't split the horses. As the boys fought, another gentleman rode up on a horse, having heard their problem. He provided them with a possible solution where they got the share they were supposed to, and no animal was harmed.

What did the mathematician tell the men?

33. Keeping Them Safe

One of the most robbed banks in the land is in Fumbletown. The unfortunate teller was often made to crack the safe, which cost the bank a lot of money. The bank manager, Mr. Perfect, was going bald as a result.

Then, one day, Mr. Perfect had a great idea: He had a nephew, Bumble, that he made the new bank teller. Now, Bumble was perfect. He couldn't remember things, so robbers couldn't make him open the safe because he couldn't remember the combination. But he was great at solving puzzles. So, when Bumble needed the combination, he had to ask for the following conundrum from Mr. Perfect, where he would be able to solve to figure out the five-digit code.

"The fourth number is four more than the second. There are three pairs of numbers that add to 11. The third number is three less than the second. The first number is three times the fifth."

What is the safe combination?

34. Just a Couple of Delinquents

There are five kids playing kickball. One of them kicked the ball so hard that they broke a window. When they are each questioned about what happened, each one of the kids gave three statements – one is a lie and two are true. The statements are:

Steve:

One of us is going to be in big trouble.

I didn't do it.

Margaret will tell who did it.

Jesse:

I hate kickball.

Amanda did it.

I didn't do it.

Mark:

Margaret doesn't know who did it.

Amanda and I are good friends.

I didn't do it.

Amanda:

I have never broken a window.

I never saw Mark before today.

Jesse lied when he said I was the one who broke the window.

Margaret:

I want to go home.

I didn't break the window.

I saw Amanda break it.

Which child broke the window?

35. The Seven Diamond Thieves

There are seven thieves who have just stolen diamonds from a diamond seller and are now running away. They hide out in the jungle for the night.

As they sleep, two wake up and decide to split the diamonds between them, but there is one diamond that is left over when they finish.

They decide to wake a third thief and then divide the diamonds between the three of them, but they still find that they have one diamond left. They do this again with the fourth, fifth, and sixth thieves.

Finally, they wake up the last thief, and are able to divide the diamonds equally amongst the seven of them.

36. The Temple Oracle

There is a man who travels to a temple to speak with an Oracle. When he arrives, there are identical men standing there. They tell him that he has to accomplish something first before he can speak to the Oracle. They tell him one of them is the Oracle, but he has to figure out which one. They also say that one of them always lies, and the other always tells the truth. He can only ask one question.

What question should the man ask?

37. Magical Grass

There is a garden store that offers magic grass. This grass comes in a single patch of sod, and it is able to double in size each day. A man decides to buy some and figure that the patch of sod can cover his garden in 14 days. So, in order to make things go faster, he buys two patches.

If he buys two patches of sod, how long will it take to cover the garden?

38. The Gold Coins of a Rich Businessman

There is a rich businessman who collects gold coins. He is very secretive about the coins, and doesn't like to share a lot of information about them. His wife comes in and asks, "How many of those coins do you have?"

After taking a moment to think, he said, "Well, if the coins were split into two groups that were unequal, and then times 32 by the difference between those numbers, it would equal the difference of the squared numbers."

She looked at her husband, puzzled. Are you able to figure out how many gold coins the merchant has based on his information?

39. A Dead Flashlight

You have a flashlight that you need to put new batteries into. You have eight batteries. Four of those are charged, and four of them are uncharged. The flashlight takes two charged batteries to work.

You aren't sure which batteries are charged, and which ones aren't. What is the least number of attempts that you could make to get the flashlight to work? One attempt is placing two batteries into the flashlight, and turning it on to see if it works.

40. Mr. Ingle's Birthday

Rhianna and Leslie are students of Mr. Ingle. Mr. Ingle's date of birth is D/M/1970, where "D" is for day and "M" is for month, and both of them know that his exact birthday has to be on one of these ten dates:
8/12/1970
8/3/1970
2/12/1970
5/9/1970
7/6/1970
5/3/1970
1/12/1970
1/9/1970
4/6/1970
4/3/1970
To help them figure out his birthday, Mr. Ingle tells Rhianna the month of his birth and then tells Leslie the day of this birth. Then he asks them, "Do you know when my birthday is?"
Rhianna replies, "I don't know, but I am positive that Mark doesn't either."
Leslie replies, "Initially I wasn't sure, but now I do."
Rhianna replies, "Oh, then now I know what it is as well."
Based on this information and the dates provided, can you figure out what the correct date of Mr. Ingle's birthday is?

41. Cocktail Hour

You head out with your four friends for some drinks to celebrate your graduation from college. You head over to your favorite bar that is famous for nine drinks: Vesper, Negroni, Manhattan,

Kamikaze, Hurricane, Grasshopper, Caipirinha, Bronx, and Aviation.

Because it is a celebration, the bartender presents you and your friends with a challenge: If you all can identify the nine cocktails after the third round of drinks, with a round being one drink each, he won't charge you. The group orders five drinks each round for three rounds. While none of you actually know anything about drinks, with the right ordering and some reductive reasoning, you are able to figure them out. How?

42. The Four Suitors

There is a very smart King who came up with a contest to find the perfect man to marry his daughter. The princess is placed inside of a 60 x 60 foot room with wall to wall carpeting. Each of the four suitors was placed in each corner with a box that they had to stand on. The goal is to be able to touch the princess' hand, so they would get to marry her.

The rules were that they couldn't step on the carpet, cross over the carpet, or hang off of anything. They also weren't allowed to use anything except for their wits and body. One of the suitors was able to figure out how to do this and marry the princess. What did he have to do?

43. He Had A Fox and Two Chickens

There once was a man who was traveling with a fox and two chickens. He comes to a river and has to figure out a way to get across it. He sees that there is a small boat that is able to carry him and only one of his animals. He can't leave the fox along with the chickens, because the fox will end up eating the chickens. How can the man make sure that the he can get himself and his animals across the river safely?

44. A Frivolous Lawsuit

There is a lawyer who is suing for one million dollars in damages due to the claims of his client:

His client said that he went to a museum where there was a painting of Marie Antoinette being beheaded. He ended up sitting on a bench and falling asleep. As he slept, he dreamed of the guillotine. When the museum closed, a guard gave him a tap on the neck just as he started dreaming of Marie Antoinette being beheaded. The tap caused the man have a fatal heart attack immediately because he thought the tap was with a guillotine blade.

Why did the case end up getting dismissed?

45. Testing The Tub

You are taking a tour of a mental asylum to learn more about how they work, as research for a book. At the end of the tour, you ask the direction what all of the criteria is that they look at to figure out if a person should be admitted to the hospital.

"Well," the director began, "We fill a bathtub up with water. Then we place a teaspoon, a teacup, and a bucket on front of the tube and ask the possible patient to empty the bathtub. We ask them, which one of these would you like?"

"Oh, I get it!" you say, "A sane person would pick the bucket, since it is bigger and would hold more water, and wouldn't take as long to empty the tub."

How does the director respond?

46. The Most Expensive Ring

Fred would like to send his girlfriend, Stacey, a very expensive ring through mail since they live very far away. The problem with this is that everything gets stolen in the mail, unless it is locked. Fred has a box with a lock for the ring. Both Fred and Stacey have a lot of locks and keys, but none of them match.

How will Tom be able to send Stacey the ring without it ending up getting stolen?

47. A Reclusive Inventor

One day, a reclusive inventor became very annoyed at all of the unwanted visitors coming through, and ringing his doorbell such that he created a new one to discourage them.

The device he created had six buttons, wired so that only one of them will actually ring the bell. If they press the wrong button, even if they press it along with the right button, the bell becomes deactivated.

Only his friends know which button to push. Everybody else has to figure it out from the description on the door. The description reads: "Exactly one of the buttons is somewhere to the left of the one, that is three to the right of one, that is somewhere to the right of the one, that is next to the one, that is two away from the one that is first mentioned. Ring only the button that is not mentioned."

What position is the correct button in?

48. The Very Selfish Son

There is a man who has a son that is very unkind and selfish. So, he decides to send his son to the market with only one coin, and tells him, "I am tired of how selfish you are. Take this coin and buy with it something for us to drink, something we can eat, something to plant, and something to feed the cows. Do not come back until you have done just this." He can only buy a single item.

What can he buy in order to fulfill his father's commands?

49. It's Surrounded by 1,000 Squares

There was a rich woman who died and gave all of her worldly possessions to her family. At the very end of the will, she said that there was one more thing she had to give away, and it was her most precious diamond.

She provided them with a clue as to where they could find it. She said, "It is in a cylinder that has 1,000 squares surrounding it." One of her grandchildren shouted out, "I can find the diamond," and quickly went and got it. Where is the diamond?

50. The Bride and Her Chickpeas

A bride once lived with her husband and mother-in-law. The bride was extremely fond of chickpeas. Her mother-in-law kept a barrel full of chickpeas in the kitchen. Every few days, the bride would go through and steal some of the chickpeas and roast them secretly, so that she could eat them.

Eventually, the amount of chickpeas in the barrel lowers to only half full, and the mother-in-law started to become suspicious of the bride because she was a new person in the household and nobody else had ever taken any of the chickpeas before. The bride knew that her new mother-in-law was suspicious of her. Once they were all cleaning the kitchen, and the bride found one of the chickpeas on the floor. She said three little words to her mother-in-law that made her mother-in-law believe that she did not like chickpeas. What were those three words?

51. The Tiger

One hot afternoon, a woman was slowly walking through a grassy field. She has enjoyed all the things she has seen. All of a sudden, she spots a ferocious tiger far off in the distance. Rather than turning back and looking for a safe place, she started running towards the tiger. Why didn't she run away?

52. Many Voices

A man hears many voices coming from another room in the house. He decides to go investigate. As he gets closer to the living room, the sounds get louder. There sounds like many people are fighting, and lots of commotion going on. He slowly opens the door. When he goes into the room, he only finds one person inside. The man isn't crazy. What happened?

53. Crazy Weather

A man was out for a drive one sunny day, when it suddenly began to rain extremely hard. In about five minutes, the rain stopped and the wind picked up. The wind gets so strong that it begins to shake the car. It seems like, just as quickly as the winds started, they stopped. The man drove home without any more problems. What was causing this crazy weather?

54. Huge Accident

There were 40 cars involved in a huge accident at the bottom of a big hill. Some cars have been overturned, some were lying on their sides, and others were resting on other cars. This pile up was so massive that even a fire truck and some military vehicles were involved in the crash too. What in the world could have caused this huge accident?

55. A Chemist

The police get a call from campus security about a murder that happened overnight in the chemistry lab at the college. A student had come in early to work on their chemistry experiment and found the professor murdered. She immediately went to find security. When the police arrived and investigated the scene, they noticed that the professor had something balled up in his hand. They gently pried his hand open. There was a small piece of paper in his grasp. They opened the paper, and on it was written a sequence of numbers. They looked at each other and shrugged. One officer called the student over.

"Hello, Miss, do these numbers mean anything to you?" They handed the paper to the student. On the piece of paper there were the following numbers: 26 – 3 – 58 / 28 – 27 – 57 – 16.

She looked at it for a moment and a smile spread across her face.

"Yes, officers, I know who the killers are."

"You know who the killers are by just looking at a series of numbers?"

"Yes, Sirs, I do."

How did the girl know who the killers were?

56. The Robbery

A couple called the police to report a robbery. The husband told the police that he thought the burglar got into their house by breaking a window. He took the policeman and showed him the broken window and the glass shattered around outside.

The police officer looked around inside and saw a few small pieces of glass near the window. The officer looked around outside and didn't notice anything out of the ordinary. He came back inside and informed the couple that he was sure that nobody had entered their house through that particular window.

How could the officer be so sure?

57. The Ship

A Japanese ship was traveling towards the open sea. The Captain of the ship went to take a shower and removed his ring. He placed it on the table in his cabin. Upon returning to his cabin, the ring was missing. He immediately called the five crew members that he suspected and asked them where they had been and what they had been doing for the past 15 minutes.

The cook stated that he was in the freezer looking for something to cook.

The engineer stated that he had been working on the engine for the generator.

A seaman stated that they were on the mast fixing the flag that was upside down.

The radio officer stated that they had been messaging the company about their arrival.

The navigations officer stated that they had been sleeping in their cabin.

The Captain immediately knew who the thief was. How did he know?

58. A Burglar

A man was being searched for in connection with many businesses being burglarized during the past several months. Surveillance cameras from these businesses showed his face clearly. The local news station showed the footage to their viewers many times. The police even put up "wanted" posters around the town to help catch these burglars. Once the police spotted this man, they didn't arrest him. Why not?

59. Free Falling

Steve lived in a fifty-storey building. There was a large meeting room in the building that many of the tenants used for parties, meetings, etc. The room could also be rented out by people who didn't live in the building. Steve was using this room to throw a surprise birthday party for his friend. He almost had everything done and was finishing up hanging the streamers. He was standing on a chair near an open window looking around at his handiwork, when he lost his balance and fell out the window. People hurriedly gathered around him expecting the worst, when he surprised them all by standing up. He wasn't hurt physically in any way. How was he able to survive falling out a window?

60. Fed-Up Pop

Joshua wouldn't stop playing video games. It didn't matter what his father said to him. His father was fed up with Joshua constantly disobeying him. He decided to take care of the problem once and for all with some elbow grease and a hammer. To Joshua's horror, he couldn't play video games, but his father could. How was Joshua's father able to play the video games?

61. The Window

Ben was found dead in his study by his friend Gary. Gary called the police. When the police arrived, they began their investigation by getting Gary's statement. Gary told them that he had decided to visit Ben today and as he walked by the windows, he wiped the frost off one of the windows and looked inside. This is when he saw Ben's body lying on the floor of the study and called the police.

The officers looked at each other, but went about their investigation.

"How did you get inside the house?"

"I have a spare key. I feed his cat and water the plants when he goes on vacation."

"We'll look around outside for a bit. You stay here in case we have any more questions."

Gary sat down and waited. The officers went outside and looked around. They stopped outside the study windows and looked at the ground and around the windows. They soon came inside and arrested Gary. Why was Gary arrested?

62. Tea

A woman was enjoying a quiet afternoon at her favorite teahouse. She was nibbling on sandwiches, drinking tea, and reading the newest novel by her favorite author. This was the first time in a long while that she has been able to just sit back, relax, and do whatever she wants to do, instead of trying to please everyone else. She had just received her third cup of tea, and was stirring sugar into it when she noticed that there was a fly in her tea.

She called the server over and told showed them the fly. They apologized and took her cup away. They went into the kitchen and returned in a few minutes.

She thanked them. A few seconds later, she yelled at the server: "You brought me the same cup of tea!" How did she know that is was the same cup of tea?

63. The Man in the Snow

Susie was out walking her dog after a recent snowfall. She saw what looked like a fallen tree in the middle of a field. What made it strange was that there weren't that many trees in this particular field. She walked closer to the edge of the field, when she realized what she was looking at: She was looking at a man lying in this snow-covered field. She called out to him several times, but got no response. She immediately called the police. Once the police arrived, they began looking around. They walked toward the body and noticed that there was one set of footprints between two parallel lines. No other tracks in the snow could be found; not even animal prints.

"Did you see anybody around?"

"No, Sir, I was just walking my dog when I noticed the body. I first thought it was a fallen tree, until I got closer. I called out to them, and when they didn't move, I called you."

"Has anyone else been around since you called us?"

"No, Sir."

"Thank you."

Once the investigation was over, the officers were quite stumped. They couldn't figure out what in the world could make tracks like that. The man had died of a gunshot wound to the back of the head. He couldn't have killed himself that way. There weren't any other tracks around. Even if someone walked in the exact same tracks as his, there would be tracks leading away from the body once he had been shot. Was the man dragging something behind him? If so, what could it be? They

34

called the coroner and had the man taken to the county morgue. They packed up their stuff and went back to the station. It wasn't until later that day, after they had been to the coroner's office to get their official report, that they finally realized who they needed to be looking for.

Who do the police need to be looking for?

64. Dangerous Routes

Peter's Trucking is a company that has delivered goods to and from the town's businesses for many years. Peter's business stays busy. His trucks are driven on the same roads and routes each day without any problems. Peter decided this year to begin receiving and delivering goods on Christmas to earn some additional money. Once Christmas rolls around, Peter sends out some drivers to the businesses who are open today. Later on in the day, Peter got a call that one of his drivers had hit a bridge and damaged the truck very badly. How can this happen if his drivers have used the same exact route without any problems?

65. Sand Bags

Each day, a man crosses a border on a bicycle. He is always carrying two bags of sand. The officers at the border receive a tip off that this man is smuggling items across the border. The officers decide to check on him each time he crosses. They pour each bag of sand out into a bucket and go through it, but find nothing. They pour it back into the bags and send him on his way. They do this every day for two months. They inspect the bags every time, and all they keep finding is sand. They finally give up and leave the man alone. Was the man smuggling, and if so, what was he smuggling?

66. Going in Circles

A man gets up at five each morning to go to work. He takes a shower, which takes him 15 minutes. It takes him another 15 minutes to get dressed. He checks his briefcase before leaving the house to make sure that all his papers are inside. This takes about two minutes. He starts his car and lets it warm up for five minutes. The drive to work takes him about two hours if there isn't a traffic jam. Today has been a good day, and he has made it in record time. Traffic slows the closer he gets to his building. When he gets close enough, he begins driving in circles. He drives in circles four times before he finally parks. This takes him another two minutes. He finally enters his building and starts his day. Why does the man drive in circles four times?

67. A Dark Room

Howard is sitting at home alone. He is bored and decides to go do something. He calls up some friends and they all agree to meet him. They meet at the local movie theatre and get tickets for the newest blockbuster. They all grab snacks and make their way into their theatre. They talk for some time before the lights begin to dim. They are all engrossed in the movie when all of a sudden, Howard stops breathing and he can't ask for help. His friends are completely unaware of his dilemma. A few minutes later, he is about to breathe and talk again. They finished watching the movie without any other problems. They left the movie theatre and went back to their normal lives. What happened to Howard during the movie that caused him not to be able to breathe or speak?

68. Thief

A woman has been seen going into a big box store each day. She is inside for about an hour, and comes out with a shopping cart full of stuff. She empties the cart and returns to the store. Once again, she is inside for several hours and leaves again with another shopping cart full of stuff. She does this several more times a day. She is never seen going through a register or paying for anything. No one has ever tried to stop her, and never calls security on her. She has been seen doing this for at least five days each week without anything being said or done. How is she getting away with this?

69. Mysterious Murder

Shirley and Glenda share an apartment. Glenda works during the night and Shirley works during the day. Their apartment is very tiny. It only has one tiny window that lets in just a bit of light and a breeze if they are lucky. It isn't big enough for a small animal to get through. The room isn't big enough for any furniture, so they sit and sleep on the floor. Since they work different shifts, Glenda sleeps when Shirley is at work, and Shirley will sleep while Glenda works. If they are ever home together, they have to sit with their backs on opposite walls with their legs going in opposite directions. They don't even have room for a table and chair. Glenda comes home one morning to find Shirley hanging from the ceiling. She immediately calls the police. She is sitting in the hallway when the police arrive. Glenda stands when the police come up to her. She extends her hand and introduces herself. "Hi, I'm Glenda. My roommate is in there." She points to the door.

One officer shakes her hand and introduces himself, "Hi, I'm Lieutenant Kevin Briggs. This is Paul Grissom and Lisa Brass. Has anyone been in or out of this room since you found your roommate?"

"No, Sir, I've been sitting right here since I got home from work. No offense, but you aren't all going to fit inside. There might be room for only one of you. It is a very small apartment. If we didn't work different shifts, we probably couldn't survive in there."

Officer Brass goes inside. She sees the body hanging from the ceiling. The rope had been tied to the ceiling joist. The sleeping bag was rolled up in one corner of the room. There was a puddle on the floor underneath the body. She takes a vial out of her bag and gets a sample of the water. Upon smelling it, she knew it wasn't urine. It seemed to be just plain water. She eases by the body and checks the rest of the room. The room is only a six by six room. The only thing this room had going for it was the ceiling height. It had a ten foot ceiling. She doesn't see anything else in the room. She goes back out into the hallway.

"This was the only thing I found in there, Lieutenant." She hands him the vial of water. He removes the cap and smells. He looks into the room for a moment.

"Well, it is obvious that she committed suicide."

How did the Lieutenant know that Shirley had committed suicide?

70. Tube Torture

A woman and her husband are fighting their way through a crowd of people. They have to go through this huge machine that determines if they can go farther into this huge building. Some people go through this machine without any problems, while other people set off an alarm. If the alarm sounds, you have to go stand to the side while more people gather around you. They run another smaller machine up and down your body while poking and prodding around in all your belongings. The woman and her husband get through this machine without setting off any alarms, and they proceed farther into the building. There are many boxes on the walls that change what they say on them from time to time. The husband goes up to one of these boxes, looks at it for a minute, and leads his wife further into this building. She is becoming more and more distraught by the minute. He leads her to a hallway where a lady is standing. He hands the lady two rectangles. The lady looks at them, hands them back to the man and motions for them to go into this long tunnel. His wife is clearly shaken by this point. She is on the verge of hysterics by now. He takes her hand as he leads her into a huge metal tube and she is struck with overwhelming fear. She holds her husband's hand extremely tight and shakes violently. Her husband holds her gently but he isn't affected in any way. In a few hours, her husband tells her it's time to go and her torment ends. What was wrong with this woman?

71. Heaven

There was a man who passed away and found himself in heaven. There were hundreds of thousands of others there, too. Everyone was naked and all looked like they did when they were 21. He tried to find somebody he knew. There were two people he knew. They were Adam and Eve. How could he possible know this?

72. The Arm

One man received a package. He looked inside, and then packed it up and sent it to somebody else. This man looked the arm over and then buried it in the woods. Why?

73. Who Did It?

There are five friends. Their names are: Niles, Martin, Maxwell, Steve, and Tyler. One of these five men shot and killed one of the others. The police have gathered together some clues:

- Niles ran in the Boston Marathon yesterday with another friend who is innocent.

- Maxwell is a computer consultant at the top of his field, who would like to install Steve's new computer next week.

- Martin wanted to be a farmer before he moved.

- The person who committed the murder had his leg amputated a few months ago.

- Steve met Tyler just six months earlier.

- Tyler has been hiding since the crime.

- Niles used to be a heavy drinker.

- Steve and Maxwell built the last computers they had together.

- The person who committed the murder is a brother to Tyler. They grew up in Nashville.

Knowing these facts, can you figure out who the killer is?

74. Smuggling Ring

Detective Jill Plunkett has been working on a smuggling ring for several months now. She is getting very close to finding the main man behind these smuggling operations. She was last seen yesterday having lunch with her friend Christy Patterson. They were eating at the new Italian restaurant down the block from Christy's office. Jill was supposed to meet Christy after work today to help her pick out a new outfit for her date on Friday night. When Jill didn't show up, Christy tried calling her cell phone, but it just went straight to voice mail. She then called Jill's office and was informed that Jill didn't come into the office today. She was going to the last known location of the smuggling boss before she came into the office today. They weren't worried, as Jill often went days without actually coming into the office. Christy asked to speak with Captain Hammond.

"Captain, I hate to bother you, but I am worried about Jill. She never misses a date, and she usually calls me every day. I haven't heard from her since yesterday. I'm afraid something has happened."

"Let me get Vince to look around her desk to see if he can find some clues as to where she might be. I'll call you right back."

"Thanks, Captain."

Vince and the Captain looked through the files on Jill's desk. The smuggling file was on top and Vince opened it. There was a list of names underneath the heading of "main suspects": Tim, Al, and Bill. The last note she had was the address of the smuggler's last known location, and a row of numbers written beside it. The numbers were 710 57735 5508 51 7718.

"Hey, Captain, what do you make of this?"

"I don't know." The Captain pulled his reading glasses out of his pocket. As he was looking at the note, Vince got a big goofy grin on his face.

"Come on Captain, I know where to find Jill."

What had Vince figured out?

75. The Killing Dish

Two men enter a restaurant. They order the exact same dish. Once they tasted it, one man went out back of the restaurant and shot himself. Why did he kill himself?

76. Dead in a Field

There is a dead man in a field. An unopened package lies next to him. There isn't anything else in the field around him. What caused him to die?

77. The Hung Man

A man was found hanging in the middle of a large barn. There is nothing else there but the man. There was no way for him to climb the wall and move along the rafters. It was decided that the man had hung himself. How did he hang himself?

78. The Man and the Bar

A man walked into a bar and tells the bartender he would like some water. Instead, the bartender points a gun at the man. He thanks him and walks out. Why?

79. The Defense Rests

A man was arrested for killing his wife. All through the trial, he kept saying that he was innocent. During his lawyer's closing statements, he surprised everyone when he announced: "His wife is only missing. Watch the doors everyone. His wife will walk through those doors any minute now."
The whole courtroom goes silent and everyone including the jury stares at the door but the defendant and his lawyer watches the jury. After a few minutes, the lawyer states: "See, if you are positive that he killed his wife, you wouldn't be looking at the door."
The jury was sent out to deliberate. After only a few minutes, they come back with a verdict of guilty. Why did they convict him?

80. The Car

A man was found shot to death inside his car. The police couldn't find any powder burns on his clothes, which showed them that the person who killed him had to be standing outside the car. All of the windows were rolled up, and all the doors were locked. Once the car was thoroughly inspected, no one could find any bullet holes, except for the ones in the body. If all the doors were locked and all the windows were rolled up, how was the man murdered?

81. Buried Alive

An evil man didn't like his four neighbors, so he decided to bury them in the ground such their heads were the only thing above ground. These men couldn't move at all, and they could only look forward.

They were buried in a line, and one of them got separated by a wall. They are facing in the same direction. The last man can see two of his friends and the wall. The one in front of him can see one head and the wall. The next one sees just the wall. The first man sees nothing in the distance.

The evil man explains the situation to the men and tells them that he will put hats on their heads. There are two red hats and two blue hats. One man is supposed to tell the evil man what color the hat is that is on his head. If he tells him the right color, the evil man will dig them up. If he says the wrong color, they will remain where they are until they die. How can the men solve this problem?

82. The King and the Clown

There was once a kingdom. There was a clown and a king who lived in this kingdom. They absolutely hate each other, so they agreed that they would poison each other.

There are just 12 vials of poison in the entire kingdom. These are all locked in a secret room in the castle.

The poisons are numbered from one to 12. The strength of the poison depends on the number on it. If it has a high number, the poison is stronger. How it affected the body was simple – drink the poison and die. Each stronger poison will neutralize the weaker poisons. This means that the poison marked "12" will neutralize all the other poisons; number 11 will neutralize everything but 12. Basically, if you were to drink poison 11 and then drink 12, nothing is going to happen. If you were to drink poison 12 and then 11, you are going to die.

The king goes into the poison room and takes all the poisons with even numbers: 2, 4, 6, 8, 10, and 12. The clown goes in and takes what is left. They agree to meet in the throne room where they each fill one cup and hand it to the other one who drinks it down. Now, they fill the cups again for themselves, and drink it in hopes that it will save their own life.

What did the clown do so that he'll wake up the next morning but the king would be dead?

The clown and the king want to live. They want to poison the other person. There is just one dose of each poison, and they can't divide it. The poisons don't have any smell nor color, and they are of the same consistency as water.

83. Death Match

You have arrived in Dry Gulch. You have already gotten in trouble. Indigo Kid and Crazy Clyde are aiming at one another with Colt 45s. They allow you to join the death match. Bullets are in short supply, so they agree to the following rules:

- The worst shooter – which is you – will shoot first, whereas the best shot shoots last.

- Participants will only shoot in the order given until only one is left.

- If somebody gets injured, the other will finish him off by beating him with an iron rod.

- Everybody will shoot only once, when it is their turn.

What tactics can you choose if you knew that you actually hit your target on the third shot? Clyde has about a 50 percent chance and Indigo Kid never misses.

84. The Building

When Shelia went into work one morning, she saw a dead body lying under the windows on the north side of the building. It looked clear that they had committed suicide by jumping out one of the upper windows.

A detective showed up and asked Shelia some questions. She answered each one as best she could. He then asked if he could see each room on this side of the building. She went to the building manager and asked for the keys to the offices on that side. She took the detective into each office. He opened all the closed windows in that room, and flipped a coin onto the floor.

They go to the second floor, and the detective does the same thing, until they get to the last floor. They then go back down. He informs his team that this wasn't suicide – it was murder. How did he know that she was murdered?

85. The Funeral

A girl was at her mother's funeral. She met a guy that she hadn't seen before. She instantly fell in love with this guy. She tried to meet him before everyone left the funeral, but wasn't able to. She hoped that he would come through the condolence line, but he didn't. She asked everyone who was at the funeral if they knew him, but no one did. She tried to find him for weeks, but was unsuccessful. Every lead just ended with another dead end. After a few weeks, she was at her wits end when she decided to kill her sister. Why did she decide to kill her sister?

86. Who Killed Him?

Murray Moore has been found dead at his desk in his office. The police have just three suspects in mind: His business partner, Mr. Jason Bates, Mrs. Sandy Hogan, and Murray's wife, Meredith. Each one of these people visited Murray on the day he was murdered. Each of these gave the police good reasons for their visit with Murray. They found him with his watch on his right arm, a photo of his wife that had been torn up laying on the floor, and a pen in his right hand. They saw a name plate on his desk, saw that his telephone was off the hook, and his date book had been turned to July 5th. "7B91011" had been written on this date. After they found this evidence, they knew who had killed Mr. Murray Moore. Do you know who it is?

87. Family Murder

A well known couple had a murder happen in their house. Their son and daughter were home when it happened. One of the four people killed one of the others. One of them saw who did the murder. The other person helped them kill the victim.
Here are the clues that we know are true:

- The person who witnessed the murder and the person who helped aren't of the same sex.

- The person who is oldest and the person who witnessed the murder are the same sex.

- The person who is the youngest and the person who was killed aren't the same sex.

- The person who helped the killer was older than the person who was killed.

- The father is the oldest member of the family.

- The person who did the killing isn't the youngest person.

Who did the killing and who got killed?

88. The Hijacked Airplane

A robber knew some valuable jewelry was being transported on the next plane leaving for New York. The jewelry was going to be displayed in the Museum of Natural History. The robber bought a ticket and boarded the plane without any problems. There were only eight passengers on the plane, including the robber. He managed to sneak into the cargo hold, and found the jewels. He packed them away and made his way back up to the main seating area. He grabbed one of the flight attendants and demanded she take him to the pilot. Once in the cockpit, he demanded the pilot to turn the plane around. Then, the pilot told him they only had enough fuel to get to their destination, and if they turned around, they would run out of gas before they got to the next airport. He then demanded that they give him nine parachutes. The pilot nodded for the flight attendant to give him the parachutes he asked for. The robber put one on, opens the door and jumps. He left the other parachutes behind. Why did he ask for nine parachutes?

89. Crack the Code

A secret agent gave his superiors the following code during a secret mission:
MOD TIE OAT DUE AIM
The twist is that the information is just in one word, and the other words are just for show. In order to help his superiors figure out the code faster, he gave them a clue. They clue read as follows:
"If I tell you any one letter of the code, you can easily find out the number of vowels in the code word."
What is the code word?

90. A Philosophical Problem

Alvin, Bert, and George are traveling across the desert. Alvin doesn't like George and decides to kill him. He decided that the easiest way to kill George would be to poison George's water

47

supply. Because they are in the middle of the desert, George has to drink water, or he will die.

Bert has no idea of Alvin's idea to kill George, and he also decided to kill George. In order to succeed in his motive, he gets rid of all of George's water so that he will die of thirst.

George indeed dies of thirst. Are we absolutely sure that Bert killed George?

91. Window Murder

Jean was standing in front of an open window, thinking about many different things. All of a sudden, she finally decides on something, and throws it out of the window. Within ten minutes, she is dead. Connie came by to eat dinner with her. Connie sees the open window and looks inside. She sees Jean lying on the floor, dead. There is no blood, no bullet holes – nothing. Connie immediately calls the police. When the police get there, they look around outside and only see Connie's footprints, and nothing else. Jean was in perfect health, and didn't have any allergies or diseases. The police go inside and look around, and they see an object lying close to the body. They look at Jean's body and determine that Jean wasn't murdered and she also didn't commit suicide.

How did this woman die?

92. Suspicious Man

A woman was sitting in her hotel room watching television, when she heard a knock on her door. She opened the door to find a strange man standing there.

The man said, "Oh, I am sorry to bother you. I thought this room was mine."

He walked downs the corridor toward the elevator. The woman closed and locked her door. She called security and told them about the suspicious man. The security apprehended him shortly thereafter. What made her so suspicious of this man? He could have mistaken her room for his.

93. Who Killed the Player?

Action Roles
The Blocker prevents the target from doing anything.
The Redirect changes the target player.
The Save protects the target player from dying.
The Seer sees everything that happens.
The Murderer will kill the target player.
The following five people are playing:
Anthony
Matthew
Mark
Luke
John
You are Anthony. You are the Seer, and this is what you saw:

- Matthew was redirected to Mark.

- Mark was blocked.

- Luke was killed.

Who was the murderer?

94. Password Lock

A man was trying to rob a bank. He finally made it into the final vault, but this one was protected by a password. He looks all around the bank, desperately trying to find the password for this lock. He was going through the President of the bank's desk, and came across something that might help him crack the code. He was frustrated and felt that they could have just written out the password rather than putting into a puzzle form. He figured it was for this very reason that they wrote it out this way. Most of the employees probably had it memorized.

Here is what was written on the paper:

- The password is five digits.

- The fourth number is four more than the second number.

- The third number is three less that the second number.

- The first number is three times the fifth number.

- Three pairs of the numbers add up to 11.

Can you help him figure out the password?

95. Murder at School

It was the first day of school when a young girl was found raped and murdered in one of the girls' restrooms. The girl that found her ran to the office and told the principal. The principal immediately called the police. The police asked if any of the teachers were present between 7:30 and 8:00 a.m. According to the time clock, there were four male teachers and three female teachers at the school at the time of the murder. The police ask each one what they were doing during this time span. The females were immediately ruled out as suspects, since the girl had been raped. They asked the four male teachers to explain what they had been doing during the time of the murder.

- Paul, who is a history teacher, stated he was in the teachers' lounge reading the morning paper.

- Neil, who is a math teacher, stated he was checking math papers.

- Rick, who was a science teacher, stated that he was locked in his room because his wife left him.

- Christopher, who is an English teacher, stated that he had been taking his wife to her job and had only arrived at school right at 8:00.

The police immediately knew who the killer is. Who raped and killed the young girl?

96. Hercule Poirot Murder

An evil serial killer would kidnap people and force them to play a game with him. In the game, he would put two pills in the middle of the table. One pill would be a normal pill. The other was filled with poison.
The victim gets to choose their pill first, and the killer takes the other one. They swallow the pills down with some water at the same time. The kidnapped victim would die every time.
One day, the killer didn't realize who he was kidnapping, and he took Hercule Poirot. When he began the game, Poirot was able to solve the puzzle of the two pills, and was able to stay alive. How did he figure it out?

97. The Snow Ball

Charles was sitting in his living room reading the paper by the fire one snowy night. A snowball suddenly breaks through his window. He looked out the window to see three of his neighbor's children running around the corner. Their names are: Casey, Arnold, and Mark Edwards.
Charles found a note the next day taped to his door. The note read: "? Edwards. He's the one who broke your window."
Which Edwards' brother does Charles need to talk to about the broken window?

98. Friday the 13th

Most people think that Friday the 13th is a very unlucky day.
Could it be possible that there isn't any Friday the 13ths in an
entire year? How many Friday the 13ths could we have in a
year? Can you figure out how to calculate it?

99. The Monkey, Dog, and Cat

A monkey, a dog, and a cat were stolen. The police caught
three suspects: Solomon, Elijah, and Joseph. We do know that
each one of these people stole an animal. What we don't know
is who stole which animal. Here are the statements that each
suspect gave to the police:
Solomon stated that Joseph stole the cat.
Elijah stated that Joseph stole the dog.
Joseph stated that they were both lying. He claimed he didn't
steal the dog or the cat.
The police found discovered that the monkey stealer had lied.
The cat stealer told the truth. Can you figure out which suspect
stole what animal?

100.   The Killing House

The police had been called to Lady Isabella's house. She had
been found dead by the cook when they came into work this
morning. The cook called the police immediately. The police had
been in the house for some time, looking everywhere for clues
of any kind. Six officers ran into the parlor, each holding a piece
of paper. On each note was written the exact same thing: "The
clues are where you will find the notes."
The Lieutenant asked each officer where they had found the
note. He asked if there were any other clues around where the
notes were found. The officers all replied that nothing else could
be found. Here is where the notes were found:
One note was found on the piano.

One note was found in the attic.
One note was found on a mirror.
One note was found in an envelope.
One not was found in the living room.
One note was found under an ashtray.
The Lieutenant asked for the servants to come into the parlor and to line up. He asked each one to state their name. Here are the servants:
Susie is the upstairs maid.
Earl is the driver.
Pamela is the cook.
Harold is the butler.
Mary is the downstairs maid.
Kaye is Lady Isabella's personal assistant.
The Lieutenant knew immediately who the killer was. How did he know?

101.   Polygamy

There was a man in a nearby town who married 20 women, but was never charged with polygamy. Why not?

Puzzle Answers

1. He Lives on the 12th Floor

He is a dwarf. He is unable to reach the upper buttons in the elevator, but when there is somebody else in the elevator, he can ask them to press his floor's button, and when it is raining he can use his umbrella to press the button.

2. Burning Fire

He takes a branch and lights it on fire, and then lights the east side of the island on fire. He lets the wind blow the fire across, and then hides in the burned part.

3. A Recorded Message

The officers are able to figure out that he was actually murdered, because the man couldn't rewind the tape if he was dead.

4. A Locked Storeroom

While you were working in the storeroom, the murderer changed the padlock out for one he had the key to, which was identical to yours. When you locked everything up, you didn't notice a difference, because you didn't need your key.
When you left, the murderer opened the storeroom, placed the dead body inside, and then replaced his padlock with your original one. Then, the next morning, you opened it with your key.

5. A Coin in a Glass Bottle

He would push the cork all the way inside of the bottle and then take the coin out.

6. The Wish of a Servant

"My wish is that my mother gets to see her grandson swinging on a swing made of gold."

7. 100 Coins

You would split the coins into a group of 90 and a group of 10. You would then flip over all of the coins in the group of ten. Once the lights are turned on, you would realize that there are an equal number of heads-up coins in both groups. This will always work.

Let's look at an example so that you can see how it works. If there are three coins in the group of 90 coins that are heads-up, then the group of 10 has seven coins heads-up and three tails-up. When you flip over the group of 10 coins, it would give you three heads-up coins, and seven tails-up coins.

8. A Sunday Morning Murder

The police realized that the murderer had to be the maid, because the mail doesn't run on Sundays.

9. A Romantic Trip

The travel agent told the detective that Mr. Walbush bought two plane tickets, but only one return ticket.

10. The Man in the Baggy Suit

If the murderer had come up behind him and shot him, he would have been shot in the back and not in the stomach.

11. The Cottage Life

The police officer believes that the newspaper deliverer is the killer. Since the paper hadn't been delivered since Monday, it would mean that they knew that nobody was going to read it.

12. Came Up a Little Short

She came up short four dollars because she read "86" upside down.

13. The Bamboo Pole

Scott ended up dying of carbon dioxide poisoning. The pole was five feet long, but only was the size of a quarter. The first time that he breathed in through it, he only took in oxygen. Then when he breathed out, the air was not able to travel the whole five feet before he had to take another breath in. He would end up just breathing back in what he exhaled. Before long, all he was going to be breathing in was carbon dioxide. This means that his cause of death was CO_2 poisoning. Dr. Rage was the one who said that he should use the pole; therefore he was the one who caused his death. Rage is a doctor, so he knows that CO_2 can kill people Therefore, Rage murdered Scott. His motive was the money in the will.

14. Three Switches, One Bulb

For the answer, let's name the switches A, B, and C.
You turn A on, and keep it on for five minutes. You turn A off, and then turn B on. You never turn on C.
You then walk into the room. If the light is on, then you know that switch B controls it. If it is off, you touch the light to see if it's warm. If it is warm, then it is controlled by switch A. If it isn't warm, then it is controlled by switch C.

15. Poisoned Juice

You have to take a minimum of ten sips. You remove one drop of liquid from 500 of the bottles and take a sip. If this mixture tastes bitter, then you know it is one of those 500 bottles. Then, you take a drop out of 250 bottles, then 125, and you continue until you have it down to only a single bottle.

16. Hotel Room

She becomes suspicious because the man knocked on the door. If he had truly thought it was his room, he wouldn't have knocked. There is a good chance that he was looking to rob the room, and knocked to make sure nobody was in there.

17. A Mysterious Death

Both Bill and Shane had drinks that had ice cubes that had been poisoned. Shane drank both of his drinks so quickly that the ice was never given the chance to melt and release their poison. Since Bill sipped on his drinks, the ice melted and he was the only one that got poisoned.

18. A Kidnapped Child

This riddle is based on a true story from Taiwan. Once the rich man reached the telephone booth, he discovered that there was a carrier pigeon in a cage. There was a message attached to the leg of the bird, telling him to place the diamond in a small bag which had been placed around the neck of the pigeon and then release the bird. Once the man did this, the police were powerless to follow the bird, as it flew across the city back to its owner.

19. The Poisoned Apple

Samantha had placed poison on one side of the knife. When she cut the apple, it transferred the poison to only one half of the apple.

20. Three Rosebushes

The wizard took the rosebushes to her home at night, and then took them back to his garden the next morning. This means that she was the only rosebush that didn't have dew on it.

21. A Dead Boyfriend

He noticed that there were some faint shadows on the envelope's surface. As he looked closer, he noticed the imprint of the words, "Happy Birthday, Friend." The ex-boyfriend forgot that the pencil will leave an impression on the paper underneath.

22. The Logical Cannibals

His last words were, "You are going to kill me slowly."
With this statement, if the cannibals view the statement as true, they would have to kill him quickly, but then this makes the statement false.
On the other hand, if they thought it was false, then they would have to kill him slowly, which would make the statement true.

23. The Six Grave Plots

This could happen if there are two widows who both have a son, and each one marries the son of the other, and these new relationships creates a daughter, it works out.
Let's say that you have the first widow, W1, who has a son, S1. Then there is a second widow, W2, who has a son, S2.
W1 marries S2 and have a daughter, D1. W2 marries S1 and they have a daughter, D2.
This means that we have:
2 Grandmothers (W1, W2) with their 2 Granddaughters (D2, D1)
2 Husbands (S1, S2) with their 2 Wives (W2, W1)
2 Fathers (S1, S2) with their 2 Daughters (D2, D1)
2 Mothers (W1, W2) with their 2 Sons (S1, S2)
2 Maidens (D1, D2) with their 2 Mothers (W1, W2)
2 Sisters (D1, D2) with their 2 (Half) Brothers (S1, S2)

24. The Traveling Monk

There is a point on the trail where the monk would have occupied the same spot at the same time on each trips. If you were to have two monks walk the trail at the same time, one starting from the top and the other from the bottom, there is going to be a point that their paths cross. This is the point.

25. Her Lazy Daughter

If the daughter wants to get her mother's money, she needs to choose envelope one. The first two statements are the false statements, and the only true one is statement three.
If the check was in the first envelope, then the first two statements are false and the third statement would be true.
If the check was in the second envelope, then both the first and second statements would be true.
If the check was in the third envelope, both the first and third statements would be true.

26. An Ancient Temple Mystery

The idols were, from left to right: The God of Diplomacy, The God of Falsehood, and The God of Truth.
Truth couldn't be the one on the left, because that one said that Truth is positioned in the middle. Truth couldn't have been the center as well, because the idol told the man that the Diplomacy was in the center. That means that Truth can only be seated at the right. Since the idol on the right, Truth, said that Falsehood is in the center, we can figure out the positions.

27. A Servant Has Gone Missing

When the first servant reports in, the King writes down that servant's number. Then when the next servant comes in, he will add that servant's number with the last number. He will continue to do this until all 99 servants have checked in.
The King knows that every number from 1 to 100, when added together, equals 5050, so all he has to do is subtract the number he has after his servants have checked in, and he will be given the number of the missing servant.

28. The Murder of His Ex-Wife

Mark is guilty because when he ran into the hospital, he screamed, "Who shot her?" But when he is being questioned by the detective, he says that the only information that he could get from the hysterical maid was that she had been taken to the hospital. The only way that he would have known she had been shot is if he did it himself, or had somebody do it.

29. Mislabeled Boxes

To do this in one step, you would pull a marble out of the box that has been labeled as "Mixed." We know that all of the boxes are mislabeled, so if you pull out a red marble from the box labeled "Mixed," then that box is full of red marbles. We could then place the label marked "Red" on the box. That would mean that the box the was originally labeled as "Red" would have to be "Blue" and the box labeled "Blue" would have to be "Mixed." The opposite would be true if you pulled a blue marble out of the box labeled "Mixed."

30. The Five Suspects

Stacey is the killer.
If we start by assuming that Ralph is the killer, then that would mean his statement is one of the lies. That would make Steven's statement true. It would also make all of the other statements true as well. So that means Ralph couldn't have done it because only three statements can be true.
We could do the same for Jackie if she was the murderer. That would make her statement false, as well as Stacey's statement. But that would also make Ralph's statement false, so that means Jackie couldn't have done it either.
But, if Stacey is the murderer, that would make Ralph's statement false, Jackie's true, Barrett's false, Steven's true, and Stacey's true, giving us the right amount of true and false statements.

31. Their Five Jealous Husbands

It is clear that there will have to be an odd number of crossings, and if the husbands weren't jealous, they could all make it over in nine crossings. But since the wives can't be left in the company of another man with her husband there, this adds two extra crossings. So they would do it in 11 crossings.

We will go over how they could have chosen to do it.

Remember: The letters are the husbands, and the numbers are the wives.

Wives 1, 2, and 3 take the boat over and drop off 1.

2, and 3 return and pick up 4.

2, and 3 stay with 1, and 4 rows the boat back.

4 gets off the boat and A, B, C get in the boat.

A and B get out of the boat, and wife 3 gets in the boat with her husband C. Right now we have husband A and B with their wives 1 and 2.

C and 3 go back across. 3 gets out of the boat and D and E get in the boat.

C, D, and E cross and get out.

2 takes the boat back across and picks up 3 and 4.

They cross and 4 gets out.

2 and 3 go back across to get 5.

2, 3, and 5 cross and everybody is back together.

32. His 17 Horses

The advice that the man gave the boys was to add his horse to their horses, so that they had a total of 18 horses.

This would mean that the oldest would get 9 horses (1/2)

The middle would get 6 horses (1/3)

The youngest would get 2 horses (1/9)

Then there would be one horse left over, and that would be the mathematician's horse.

33. Keeping Them Safe

The combination would have to be 65292.

Since the third number must be three less than the second, and the fourth is four more than the second, this leaves you with only three possible combinations for the middle three numbers. These are -529-, -307-, and -418-.

With the criteria for the first and fifth number, the only possible combinations for these numbers are 0 0, 3 1, 6 2, and 9 3. You can find the solution by combining these sets of numbers with the other criteria that there are three two number combinations that add up to 11.

34. Just a Couple of Delinquents

Mark was the one that broke the window.

Amanda's first and third statements have to be true. If she did break the window, the statements would have been false, but we know only one statement can be false. Therefore, Amanda's statement two is the lie.

Using this information, you can go through it and figure out which one of the children's statements are true or false.

Since we know that Amanda's second statement was the lie, which means Margaret's statement one and Jesse's statement one would have to be a lie. Steve's statement two has to be a lie as well, since Margaret didn't tell who actually did it. The last person we are left with is Mark.

35. The Seven Diamond Thieves

They would have to have stolen 301 diamonds.

You have to figure out a number that is a multiple of 7 that isn't a multiple of 2, 3, 4, 5, and 6. 60 is the least common multiple, so the answer has to be one greater than the multiple of 60.

6 +1 = 61, but it isn't a multiple of 7

6 x 2 +1 = 121, but it isn't a multiple of 7

6 x 3 + 1 = 181, but isn't a multiple of 7

6 x 4 +1 = 241, but isn't a multiple of 7

6 x 4 + 1 = 301, it is a multiple of 7

36. The Temple Oracle

The man would have to ask, "If you were the other one, who would you say is the Oracle?"
If he asked the one who told the truth, he would have to point to the one who tells a lie. If he asked that to the one who lied all the time, he would have to point at himself.

37. Magical Grass

It would take him 13 days to cover his entire garden using two patches of sods. The reason is that each patch of the sod will have to cover half of his garden. Since we know that one patch of sod will completely cover his garden in 14 days, and the sod doubles in size each day, that means the sod would cover half of his garden in 13 days. This means that it would take 13 days for each patch to cover half of his garden.

38. The Gold Coins of a Rich Merchant

The merchant would have to have 32 gold coins.
To prove this, divide the 32 coins into two unequal numbers. We'll say five and 27.

$23(27 - 5) = (27^2) - (5^2)$

$704 = 729 - 25$

If the two unequal numbers were 22 and 10, then:

$23(22 - 10) = (22^2) - (10^2)$

$384 - 484 - 100$

Alternatively, we can represent the two numbers by x and y.
This means that we would have $32(x - y) = x^2 - y^2$
$x^2 - y^2$ can also be written as $(x - y)9x+y)$
This then makes the equation $32 = x + y$
$x + y$ will tell you the total number of gold coins.

39. A Dead Flashlight

You are going to have to have eight attempts in order to figure out the two working batteries.

You would divide the batteries into three groups. There would be two groups of three, and one group of two. When you do this, you will guarantee that at least of these groups are going to have two working batteries in them.

Both of the groups of threes have three possible combinations of two batteries, and there is only one combination in the group of two. That means that, at most, you will have to try seven times.

40. Mr. Ingle's Birthday

Mr. Ingle's birthday would have to be 1/9/1970.

As said in the riddle, "D" and "M" represents the day and month of his birth respectively.

Rhianna can only know the date if Mr. Ingle told her a unique month. In the options, there aren't any unique months. Leslie can only know his birthday if he is provided with a unique day. There are two unique days: seven and two. Since Rhianna can ensure that Leslie doesn't know, we know that Leslie doesn't have a month that corresponds with a unique day. So that gets rid of June and December. This leaves us with March and September:

4/3/1970
5/3/1970
8/3/1970
1/9/1970
5/9/1970

That would mean Leslie would have to guess the day to be either 1, 4, 5, or 8. Since Leslie can figure out the date, the day must be unique. If Leslie had been told one, she would know it is 1/9/1970. If she was given a four, it would be 4/3/1970. If she had been told an eight, it would be 8/3/1970. But she couldn't have been given a five, because it is not unique.

This takes it down to

4/3/1970

8/3/1970

1/9/1970

And since Rhianna is able to figure out the birth date at this point, this means that there must be one unique month value which would eliminate any in March, leaving the only answer as 1/9/1970.

41. Cocktail Hour

During the first round, you order two Grasshoppers, a Caipirinha, a Bronx, and an Aviation. The Grasshopper can now be identified.

During the second round, you order two Manhattans, a Kamikaze, a Hurricane, and an Aviation. Now the Manhattan and Aviation can be identified.

During the third round, you order two Vespers, a Negroni, a Hurricane, and a Bronx. Now the Negroni, Kamikaze, Caipirinha, Hurricane, Bronx, and Vesper can be identified.

42. The Four Suitors

All he had to do was to ask the princess to walk over and touch his hand.

43. He Had A Fox and Two Chickens

To do this, the man would have to take the fox over and return alone. He then gets a chicken and takes it across. He leaves the chicken, places the fox back in the boat, and takes the fox across. He then leaves the fox on the other side, gets the second chicken, and takes the second chicken across. He then goes back over by himself and gets the fox. He and the fox return to the other side and everybody can go home alive.

44. A Frivolous Lawsuit

If the man ended up having a fatal heart attack, then he would have died. This means that there would be no way of knowing what he was dreaming of.

45. Testing The Tub

The director turns to you and says, "No. A sane person would simply walk over to the tub and pull out the plug. Where would you rather we put you – near the heater or the window?"

46. The Most Expensive Ring

Fred will first place the ring into the box and lock it up with one of his locks. Once Stacey receives the package, she will then place one of her own locks on the box and then send it back to Fred. When Fred receives the package, he will remove his lock from the box and then send it back to Stacy. She will then be able to unlock her lock and get the ring.

47. A Reclusive Inventor

The correct one would be fifth from the left.
We know the right one isn't mentioned in the description, so if we find where the ones mentioned are located, the right one is the only one left.
If the buttons mentioned are A B C D E, we can start with the best relation – that is, B is three to the right of C. Since a position is not able to have two letters, the deduction would show that from left to right, the buttons would have to be D E C A B. So that would mean that the doorbell is fifth from the left.

48. The Very Selfish Son

He could have bought a watermelon. They can drink the juice, eat the pulp, plant the seeds, and feed the rind to the cows.

49. It's Surrounded by 1000 Squares

She hid her most precious diamond in a roll of toilet paper.

50. The Bride and Her Chickpeas

All she had to say was, "What is this?" If she doesn't know what a chickpea is, then why would she be the one stealing them?

51. The Tiger

The lady had spent the day strolling around the local zoo. She had always dreamed of seeing the tigers up close, so when she spotted their enclosure, she ran toward it. She wasn't scared because she knew they could not get to her. She was very excited to finally get to see a tiger in person.

52. Many Voices

When he opened the door, his son was watching a cop show on television. All the voices and commotion was coming out of the television set. The cops were chasing a car around town with their sirens blaring. There were people yelling and screaming, guns being shot – all sorts of crazy things were going on. He politely asked his son to turn the volume down before he scared everyone else in the house.

53. Crazy Weather

The man decided at the last minute that he needed to wash his car, so he drove his car into a drive-through car wash. As the car went through the wash and rinse cycles, it was "raining". During the dry cycle, as the blowers were blowing the car dry, this was when he endured all the torrential winds. Once his car was cleaned, which took about ten minutes, he drove home.

54. Huge Accident

This accident was caused by a child – a child's wonderful imagination, that is. The cars, trucks, military vehicles, fire trucks, and other vehicles were all part of this little child's day of fun in the sun. The big hill was created by a pile of dirt that was created by a pail, some dirt, and a shovel. If you leave a child alone, they will find many ways to entertain themselves.

55. A Chemist

The student informed the officers that the numbers on the paper corresponded to the atomic numbers that were found on the periodic table of elements: 26 = Fe, 3 = Li, 58 = Ce to spell "Felice". The other set of numbers spelled: 28 = Ni, 27 = Co, 57 = La, 16 = S which spells out "Nicolas". They were able to find the two men and bring them to justice.

56. The Robbery

The officer knew that nobody had broken that window from the outside, because the majority of the glass was found outside. If someone on the outside of the house had broken the window, there would be more glass on the inside. Therefore, no one had broken into their home.

57. The Ship

The flag couldn't have been upside down, as a Japanese flag is just a red circle on a white background. It looks the same both upside down and the right side up. The seaman was the thief.

58. A Burglar

The man that was wanted had already been arrested, and he was sitting in jail. When the officers noticed that he had been arrested, they wanted to get his statement about what took place during the robbery. They couldn't arrest him again; they could only talk to him.

59. Free Falling

Steve was able to survive the fall out the window because the meeting room that he was decorating for the surprise party could be found on the first floor. The only thing that got hurt was his pride.

60. Fed-Up Pop

Joshua's dad used a hammer and hung a shelf in Joshua's room that was too high for Joshua to reach even when using a chair. Joshua's dad then placed the video game controllers and console on the shelf out of Joshua's reach. The dad could play the video games any time he wanted, since he could reach the console and controllers.

61. The Window

Gary was arrested because when he stated that he wiped the frost off the window and looked in, they knew he was lying because frost will form on the inside of a window since it's colder outside. Gary couldn't have wiped the frost from the window. The officers also didn't find any footprints outside the study window either. Gary let himself in and killed his friend.

62. Tea

When she took a sip of tea, the tea tasted sweet. If they had poured out the tea with the fly in it and filled up a new cup of tea, the tea wouldn't have been sweetened. She knew it was the same tea because she had already put honey and lemon in her tea. They had only removed the fly from her tea instead of giving her a new cup altogether.

63. The Man in the Snow

While they were at the morgue, they saw a man rolling into the building in a wheelchair and he left two tracks exactly like what they saw in the field. They knew then that they needed to investigate the dead man's acquaintances who were in a wheelchair.

64. Dangerous Routes

On Christmas day, most of the businesses that used Peter's company weren't open. Once the truck made its final delivery, and since it didn't have anything to pick up, it was empty. While returning to the shop, because the truck was empty, it had a higher profile, and hit the bridge.

65. Sand Bags

This man was very clever. It is true that he crossed the border on a bicycle carrying sandbags every time. Yes, the sand was inspected and nothing was found in the sand. If the officers had been paying closer attention, they would have noticed that the man was riding a different bicycle every time he crossed the border. He had been smuggling bicycles across.

66. Going in Circles

The reason the man drives his car in circles is because his building is located in the busiest part of town. He has to park his car in a nearby parking garage. He couldn't find a parking space until he made it to the fifth floor of the garage. Therefore, he had to drive in circles four times before he found an empty parking space.

67. A Dark Room

While they were watching the movie enjoying popcorn, candy, and soda, Howard goes to take a drink of his soda. He doesn't like using straws so he takes the lid off his cup and takes a big gulp. An ice cube slides down his throat along with the soda and gets stuck. For a few minutes, Howard was unable to breathe or speak. He didn't get alarmed as he knew that it being a piece of ice, it would melt soon and he would be fine. That was why he didn't ask his friends for help.

68. Thief

The woman is part of the janitorial staff at the big box store. She periodically goes through the store, emptying trash cans and gathering up empty boxes. Once her shopping cart gets full, she takes it outside to empty it into either the dumpster or the recycling bins. She then goes back inside and brings more trash out. This is why she doesn't have to go through a register or pay for anything. No one tries to stop her or calls security because she is just doing her job.

69. Mysterious Murder

The room was too large for Shirley to have been able to hoist herself up the walls and hang herself that way. The puddle that was found under her was from a block of ice she had been standing on. She had time to climb up on the ice, tie the rope around a ceiling joist and her neck before the ice melted, thus, hanging herself.

70. Tube Torture

The woman has a debilitating fear of flying. She has to travel to see a relative who is dying. This only adds to her emotional upheaval. As her husband takes her through the airport, she gets more and more nervous. By the time they get to the gate, she is visibly shaken. Once she enters the plane, she is overwrought with fear, and her husband tries to console her. The flight lasts a few hours, and when they get to their destination, she can leave the plane.

71. Heaven

They were the only ones without bellybuttons. Since they weren't born of woman, they didn't have umbilical cords, and so they wouldn't have had navels.

72. The Arm

The men were stranded on an island. They desperately needed to eat, so they agreed that they would each amputate their left arm. They made an oath that everyone would have their left arms amputated. One of them was a doctor, so he amputated the arms. Shortly thereafter, they ended up getting rescued. They took a binding oath, so he had to amputate his own arm and send it to them.

73. Who Did It?

Maxwell killed Martin. Here is how to figure it out:

- Tyler can't be the murderer since his brother is the murderer.

- Niles couldn't be it because he was running in the marathon, and the murderer had an amputated leg, so he wouldn't be running that fast.

- Steve can't be the killer, because he had just met Tyler, and Tyler grew up with the killer.

- That leaves us with Maxwell and Martin.

Because Maxwell is still living and wants to work on a computer the next week, this places him as the killer. Martin and Tyler didn't grow up together. We know that Tyler, Niles, Maxwell are all still alive. Steve has to be living, since Maxwell is working on his computer next week. This determines that Maxwell had to kill Martin.

74. Smuggling Ring

Bill is the smuggler that Jill has been after. While the Captain was looking at the note, Vince was looking at it upside down. Jill had written the note in numbers. If you look at the numbers closely, they look like letters, and they form a sentence. They message read: "Bill is boss. Sells oil."

75. The Killer Dish

The dish the two men ordered was albatross. They had been stranded on an island years earlier. Once the man put albatross in his mouth, he realized that he hadn't tasted it before. This meant the meat he had eaten wasn't albatross like he had been told by his friend who gave it to him. He had figured out that he had eaten his son's flesh, who had died right after they reached the island.

76. Dead in a Field

He had jumped out of an airplane, but his parachute didn't open. This was the unopened package near him.

77. The Hung Man

He had climbed up on a block of ice that had melted.

78. The Man in a Bar

The man had a bad case of the hiccups. The bartender realized this when he ordered the water. The bartender pulled a gun on him in order to scare the man. It actually worked and he was cured of the hiccups. The man didn't need the water anymore.

79. The Defense Rests

They knew he was guilty, because he didn't look at the door like everyone else did. He just watched to see what the jury was going to do. He thought he could trick everybody. He didn't look at the door because he knew she wouldn't be coming through it.

80. The Car

The man was sitting in a convertible car. All the windows were rolled up with the doors locked, but being in a convertible, the gunman was able to kill him without damaging the car in any way.

81. Buried Alive

If the last man can't tell the evil man the answer soon, this means that the two men in front of him have different hats. The man in front of him just says the color that isn't on the head in front of him. He will, of course, give the last man enough time to talk just in case he knew the answer.

82. The King and Clown

The King keeps poison number 12 for himself, so he can neutralize any poison that the clown gives to him. He pours poison number ten for the clown. The clown counted on this, so he kept poison 11 for himself, so that he could neutralize poison number ten. This is how he was able to survive. He knew that the King would drink poison number 12 after he gave him the first poison. The clown poured water into the cup for the King to drink first. He drinks the water and then drinks poison number 12. Since water isn't a poison, the King died.

83. Death Match

It would be best if you just shot into the air. If you shoot at Clyde and, by chance, hit him, you will die. If you shoot at Indigo Kid and hit him, there is a chance you will die before you get a chance to shoot at Clyde. If you shoot into the air, Clyde will shoot Kid because Clyde knows that Kid is a better shot. If he misses, Clyde will die. If he hits Kid, you now have a chance to shoot Clyde. You have one third of a chance to win. On your first shot, if you shoot any of the opponents, you will always be in a worse situation.

84. The Building

If she had committed suicide, there would have been a window open somewhere. Because all of the windows in all the offices on the north side of the building were closed. The detective knew immediately that the woman had been thrown out of the window, because the killer closed the window behind them when they left.

85. The Funeral

She thought that maybe he was a strange person who liked going to funerals, or maybe he worked for the funeral company. She killed her sister in the hopes that he would show up at her sister's funeral and she would finally get to meet him again.

86. Who Killed Him?

The killer was determined to be Jason Bates. The number that had been written on the calendar has been written quickly. The police matched up the numbers with the months. The "B" was actually meant to be an "8". so that gives you the numbers seven, eight, nine, ten, and eleven. These correspond with the months July, August, September, October, and November. Using their first letter, it spells J A S O N.

87. Family Murder

The Mother did the killing. This is how we figured it out:
You know from the third point, that they youngest person wasn't the victim. The fourth point tells us that the youngest wasn't the helper. The sixth point tells us that the youngest wasn't the killer. The youngest was only the one who witnessed the murder. If you make a chart of the three possible combinations, it might look something like this:
W stands for Witness, M stands for Murderer, V stands for Victim, and H stands for Helper
Oldest was the father = H, H, M
Next oldest was the mother = V, M, H

75

Next to the youngest was the son = M, V, V
Youngest was the daughter = W, W, W
If you look back at point five that the father was the oldest person. and from point two, it told us the youngest person was the daughter. Therefore, the next youngest person was the son. and the next oldest had to be the mother.
The first isn't possible, because point three stated that the victim and the youngest person were of different sexes. The third isn't possible either, because from point one, the helper and the witness are different sexes. By this knowledge, the only possibility that holds true is that the mother was the killer, and the son was killed.

    88. The Hijacked Airplane

If the pilot thought he was taking hostages, he wouldn't risk giving him faulty parachutes as this might cause an innocent person to get killed.

    89. Crack the Code

The word is TIE
Let's look a bit closer: If you were told a letter of MOD, you wouldn't be able to figure out if the number of vowels is one or two. Let's say the letter was M, and then you could associate two words with M such as MOD and AIM. AIM has two vowels, whereas MOD has just one. You could say the same about the letters D and O, too.
Basically, every word has the letters M, O, or D can be ruled out. This leaves you with TIE. If you look at the letters in TIE, you will see that it remains true for every letter of the word. And this makes it the code word.

    90. A Philosophical Problem

The answer to the question might be more philosophical than the actual question.

It is true that Bert's actions led to George's death, but it was the scarcity of water that ultimately led to his death. It could have been the circumstances that caused his demise, and not a certain person that killed him.

91. The Window Murder

Jean had been feeling bored all day, and she had been standing at her window trying to figure out something fun to do. She remembered she had a boomerang and had never used it before. She flung the boomerang out of the window. It went the maximum distance it could go, and returned back extremely fast. It hit her in the head and caused an internal injury. She died where she stood.

92. Suspicious Man

She was right to be suspicious of this man. If the man genuinely thought the room was his, he would have tried his key first, rather than knocking on the door. He could have looked at the number on his key to see if he was at the right room, rather than disturbing someone else.

93. Who Killed the Player?

John was the murderer.
The way to figure out this is:
You are Anthony and the Seer, so you would exclude yourself.
If Matthew was the killer, then Mark would have died.
You know that Mark was blocked. This keeps him from being the killer.
Luke couldn't be the killer, because he was killed.
This only leaves John.

94. Password Lock

The five digit password number is 6 5 2 9 2.
Let's go down the list to help you out:

- The fourth is four more than the second: 9 is four more than 5.

- The third number is three less than the second number: 2 is three less than 5.

- The first number is three times the fifth number: 6 is three times 2.

- Three pairs of number sum up to 11: 6 + 5 = 11, 2 + 9 = 11, and 9 + 2 = 11.

95. Murder at School

Neil raped and murdered the young girl, as he wouldn't have had any papers to be grading, as it was the first day of school.

96. Hercule Poirot Murder

He figured out that the pills weren't poisoned. The killer has been putting the poison in the water of his victims.

97. The Snow Ball

The brother that Charles should question is Mark Edwards. The note had a "?" question mark on it, so it was telling Charles to "question Mark Edwards. He broke your window."

98. Friday the 13th

First, you have to understand that a normal calendar is confusing when counting dates due to leap day. We are going to refer to them as "Undecember" and "Dodecember" of the year before. This means that the year will run from March through "Dodecember" and the leap day will be located between the different years.

Now, we just have to figure out what day the first day of March falls on. With this knowledge, the rest of the weekdays become fixed. Let's show the first weekday of the year by an "X". "X" will run from zero through six. Zero will be a Wednesday, one is Thursday, two is Friday, etc., going on up with six being a Tuesday.

You would have easily been able to make this table, which provides a possible number of "X", and shows the months that would have Friday the 13th in it:

X – Months with a Friday the 13th

0 – October

1 – April, July

2 – September, December

3 – June, "Dodecember"

4 – March, November

5 – August

6 – May, "Undecember"

In this example, we are using March the 1st of 2002, which is a Friday. For the year 2002, September and December will have a Friday the 13th.

    99. The Monkey, Dog, and Cat

Solomon stole the Monkey.

Elijah stole the Cat.

Joseph stole the Dog.

    100.   The Killing House

You have to look carefully at where the notes were found.

The first clue was on the Piano.

The second was in the Attic.

The third was on a Mirror.

The fourth was in an Envelope.

The fifth was in the Living room.

The last was found under an Ashtray.

P A M E L A. Pamela is your killer.

    101.   Polygamy

He was a priest. He married them to other men; not himself.

Connect with us on our Facebook page
www.facebook.com/bluesourceandfriends and stay tuned to our latest book promotions and free giveaways.

61 Lateral Thinking Puzzles

The Entry-Level Logic and Riddle Book
Designed for Family After-Dinner Activities

Karen J. Bun

Bluesource And Friends

This book is brought to you by Bluesource And Friends, a happy book publishing company.

Our motto is **"Happiness Within Pages"**

We promise to deliver amazing value to readers with our books. We also appreciate honest book reviews from our readers.

Connect with us on our Facebook page www.facebook.com/bluesourceandfriends and stay tuned to our latest book promotions and free giveaways.

Don't forget to claim your FREE books!

Brain Teasers:
https://tinyurl.com/karenbrainteasers
Harry Potter Trivia:
https://tinyurl.com/wizardworldtrivia
Sherlock Puzzle Book (Volume 2)
https://tinyurl.com/Sherlockpuzzlebook2

Also check out our other books
"67 Lateral Thinking Puzzles"
https://tinyurl.com/thinkingandriddles

"Rookstorm Online Saga"
https://tinyurl.com/rookstorm

"Korman's Prayer"
https://tinyurl.com/kormanprayer

"The Convergence"
https://tinyurl.com/bloodcavefiction

"The Hardest Sudokos In Existence (Ranked As The Hardest Sudoku Collection Available In The Western World)"
https://tinyurl.com/MasakiSudoku

Introduction

Thank you for purchasing *61 Lateral Thinking Puzzles: The Entry Level Logic and Riddle Book Designed for Family After-Dinner Activities.* If you are reading this, then you are in store for a lot of fun and brain teasing.

In this book, you will find a collection of word problems, riddles, and puzzles which are sure to pique your interest, and put your brainpower to the test. Now, these aren't just any ordinary brain teasers. These are logic-based puzzles, where you will have to test your understanding and knowledge of the information provided in the puzzle, along with your own knowledge and abilities.

These puzzles are a great way to stimulate conversation among friends and family. They make for great dinner conversations, especially when you are looking to mix things up a bit. These puzzles are sure to give your brain a good workout.

Please keep in mind that these puzzles do have correct answers. So, it is important to work through your conversation in order to get the right answer. In addition, it is best to develop a strategy to figure out the final answer.

For you to get the most out of this book, here are some helpful suggestions and ideas that can help you maximize the benefits that you can get while completing each of the puzzles.

First of all, one great way to go about this strategy is to jot down your ideas. You can have a brainstorming session where everyone gets a chance to present their ideas. Then, you can talk about the answer that you believe makes the most sense. Finally, you can vote on the best one. This approach works really well when you are in a group setting, especially if there is a large number of people.

Now, if you are on your own, it is always helpful to think out loud. Often, hearing yourself say something can help put things into perspective. That allows you to assess the solution that you have come up with.

Moreover, the most important thing to bear in mind is that as long as you maintain a collaborative effort, you can always find a good solution to each of the puzzles contained in this collection. Of course, two heads think better than one. So, the same goes for multiple heads. Fostering collaborative effort in solving each one of these puzzles is a great way to build trust and stimulate cooperation among family members, friends, and colleagues.

Another useful tip is to have a lead. Now, this is not so much a leader, but a lead or moderator to keep order in the conversation. The lead can make sure that everyone gets their turn to speak. That way, no one will get left out. The main purpose of having a leader is to guide the discussion so that participants do not veer off-topic. Furthermore, the lead can offer hints and helpful suggestions in case anyone gets stuck.

Leads ought to be the only ones with access to the solutions. This will take away the temptation to skip ahead and check out what the solution is. That way, each team will have to figure out their own solution(s) to each one of the puzzles in a creative fashion.

Another spin on this could be a more competitive approach. This approach works great if you have a large number of people at your gathering. The total number of participants can be divided into two groups. The lead can act as a master of ceremony who will read the problem to both teams. Then, each team is given an allotted amount of time to solve the puzzle. Each team designates a spokesperson who explains their answer. The lead is in charge of making sure that the correct answer is revealed once the discussion portion is over.

In general terms, 10 minutes per puzzle is a good amount of time to discuss a puzzle. Unless the puzzle in unusually complex, 10 minutes should suffice. Most importantly, you want to make sure that both teams have enough time for a discussion. If you feel that more time is required, then, by all means, assign more time in 5-minute increments. Make sure you don't forget to keep to the time, though!

Now, a very important warning: In the back of this book, you will find the solutions to each one of the puzzles presented herein. Please resist the temptation to go back and check out the solution beforehand. That is why it is best for the moderator or leader to be the only one with the solution in their hands.

Otherwise, you may not be able to resist the temptation of checking out the answers before you have worked out all of the possible solutions.

It is certainly worth taking the time to work out all of the possible solutions to each puzzle. It might even be that you can come up with a better solution to a puzzle than the one offered. So, don't hold back. Who knows? You might be able to come up with an even better solution.

What that in mind, let's begin!

Game Play Instructions

Instructions: Please read through each one of the puzzles presented. Then, work individually in pairs or in groups to work out the answer. Once you have come up with one, you can refer to the back of this book to check out the correct solution.

Also, using visuals such as a board, flipchart, or just a plain pen and paper will help you in working out the possible solutions to each problem. Often, using visuals will help you and your teammates get a better understanding of the problem and its possible solution(s).

Please keep in mind that there is only one answer to each puzzle. And while it is perfectly plausible to come up with more than one answer, each puzzle has been designed to have just one logical solution.

Just a friendly reminder: Don't check the official answer until you have fully worked out the puzzle. If you check the answer before you have fully discussed the issue, you won't get the most out of the exercise.

So, without further ado, here we go!

Puzzle #1 The Twins Dilemma

A family happily welcomed their new twin sons. The boys were named Rory and Cory. After about a year, the parents realized something very strange. While they both have the same mother and the same father, and they were both born in the same city and in the same hospital, it turns out that Rory and Cory were born on a different day, month, and year.

How is this possible?

Puzzle #2 How Did the Farmer Cross the River?

A farmer is walking with a sheep, a wolf, and a sack of grain. When he gets to his boat to cross the river, the farmer realizes that the sheep, the wolf, and the grain, in addition to himself, would be too much weight for the boat. So, he can only take one of the sheep, wolf, and grain, along with himself in the boat and across the river.

Thus, he needs to take one by one across the river. However, here is the catch: If he leaves the sheep and the wolf alone, the wolf will eat the sheep. If he leaves the sheep and the grain alone, the sheep will eat the grain.

Oh, what should a farmer do?

How can the farmer get all three across the river?

Puzzle #3 Mr. Jones' Math Class

In a high school, there are three girls in Mr. Jones' math class: Mary, Cindy, and Josephine. Mary speaks more softly than Cindy, and Josephine speaks more loudly than Cindy. Since the girls talk too loudly in class, Mr. Jones has decided to punish all of the students, except for the students who speak the softest. Mary has said that she speaks the softest. Josephine disagrees. So, does Mary speak softer or more loudly than Josephine?

Puzzle #4 Speaking of Math Class...

Mr. Jones' other math class took their midterms last week. After grading the math test, the average score of the students in the class is 6. Eight students scored 3 points, and the rest scored over 5 points. Assuming that the total score is 10 and 5 is a passing grade, what is the average score of all of the students who passed the test?

Puzzle #5 The Big Race in the City

The city has decided to organize a race to determine the city's fastest runner. The winner would go on to compete in the state championship. Since thousands of runners signed up, the city decided to hold elimination trials until the top four runners were left. They would then have one final heat to decide who would be the city champion.

The four runners in the competition were labeled: A, B, C, and D. As far as the results go, we know that C arrived right after B, and D arrived in between A and C.

Can you determine the order in which they crossed the finish line so that we can figure out who the city champion is?

Puzzle #6 Going on Vacation With the Bros

Six friends have decided to go on vacation together after a long semester at college. However, they can't all take the same means of transportation together as they can't afford to fly. So, they have chosen to travel in pairs on the same means of transportation. Alex won't be driving, as he will join Jack, who isn't flying. Andy is flying. Charlie is not traveling with Mike, who doesn't fly either.

Based on the previous information, can you determine what means of transportation Tom is taking?

Puzzle #7 A Family of Big Eaters

A family that lives in a quiet village has four dogs: Scout, Precious, Buddy, and Ace. Each dog is a big eater. After going over the family's budget, the parents were shocked to see how much they spend on dog food each month. So, the parents have decided to determine which dog eats the least. The dog that eats the least would stay home, while the other three would be up for adoption.

This is what they found out:

Ace eats more than Scout. Buddy eats more than Scout, but less than Precious. Precious eats more than Ace.

Which dog gets to stay home with the family?

Puzzle #8 To Shoplift or Not to Shoplift?

In a large department store, on a regular day, a woman enters, takes a shopping cart, and proceeds to fill it up to the top. Then, the lady walks out of the store without paying for anything, and without being stopped by the store's security guards. She was caught on the store's security cameras as well.

How is it possible that the lady can leave the department store without being stopped by security?

Puzzle #9 A Bit Too Much Excitement

A man is in a large, dark room having a great time. There is quite a bit of noise, but everyone is silent. Then, the man is unable to breathe or speak. The other people in the dark room do nothing help him, nor do they call for help. After a few moments, the man can breathe and speak again. He resumes having a great time, along with everyone else.

How is this situation possible?

Puzzle #10 Tell Me What You See

A local bookstore has offered free, premium memberships to its book club for the first 10 customers who successfully crack a code.

The question posed by the bookstore was:

Please look at the following image.

You have 10 seconds to indicate what it means.

Based on this information, can you solve the puzzle, and give the answer to the bookstore's customers?

Puzzle #11 Which Way Is Up?

A man lives in the penthouse of a 45-story building in a large, metropolitan city. The man is very fit and athletic. He has a great job. In the mornings, he leaves home at 7:45 and takes the elevator down to the lobby of this apartment building. However, he takes the stairs up every evening when he gets home at around 7 pm.

Why does the man take the elevator down in the morning but not up in the evening?

Puzzle #12 Going Around in Circles

A very well-respected lawyer works in a fancy office building downtown. Every morning, when she gets to her office, she needs to drive around in circles six times before she can park her car, and then proceed to make her way to her office. Sometimes, other cars are blocking her way around in circles.

Why does she have to drive around in circles every day before parking and going to her office?

Puzzle #13 That's All She Wrote

A very wealthy lady sits at her desk every month and writes two words on 60 pieces of paper every week. The pieces of paper are small but important. She must do this every week as many people are counting on her to do so.

Why would this lady write two words on 60 pieces of paper every week?

Puzzle #14 Swing and a Miss

During a baseball game, the best batter on the team has two strikes. There are no runners on the bases. On the next pitch, the batter swings and misses, thereby striking out. The batter then scrambles toward first base. He reaches first base and is called "safe" by the umpire.

So, why isn't the batter out and standing at first base?

Puzzle #15 Burning the Candle at Both Ends

Rob is a very hard worker. He's got a steady job with steady hours. So, he is happy that he has a respectable job. He has a nice family, and enjoys fishing when he gets the chance to go. He usually stays up all night. He doesn't get any sleep at all at night, but does not end up feeling exhausted in the morning. He does this on a regular basis.

How is it possible that Rob doesn't sleep at night, yet he is not exhausted in the morning?

Puzzle #16 Child's Play

There are several children playing in the playground. Two kids are in the sandbox, playing quietly on their own. One child has made 3 sand piles, and the other child has made 4 sand piles. Then, one of the kids starts talking to the other one. Both children decide that they want to make a large sandcastle. So, they figure out that the best way to make a large sandcastle is to combine their piles.

After combining their sand piles to make their castle, how many piles do they have?

Puzzle #17 Your Wishes Are My Command

There was once a very powerful wizard. This wizard could grant any wishes and desires. After a very long life, the wizard felt he was about to die. So, he called his faithful servant in his chamber. The wizard said to his servant, "My dear servant, you have served me faithfully over all of these years. I feel that I will soon leave this life. As a reward for your faithful service, I will grant you one wish".

The wizard gave his servant one day to think about this wish. So, the servant went home to his wife and told him about this. Since this couple had been childless, his wife urged him to ask his master for a child.

Then, the servant went to see his mother, who had lost her sight. After telling his mother about what his master had offered, his mother asked him to request for her sight back.

On his way back from seeing his mother, the servant thought about what he wanted. He decided that he wanted to be very rich. He decided that he wanted a lot of money to solve all of his worries.

The next day, the wizard called his servant. "My dear servant, have you decided what wish you desire?"

The servant then made one wish where he was able to get all three desires.

How is it possible to get all three wishes into a single wish?

Puzzle #18 Something's Fishy

A lovely elderly lady had a beautiful blue tropical fish. She loved this fish dearly, as it was her only companion. One day, she noticed that the fish was swimming about strangely and seemed to be sick. Since this was her beloved companion, the lady rushed her fish to the vet.

The vet took one look at the fish and said, "Come back in an hour."

The lady smiled and nodded. She left and then came back in an hour to see her beloved companion swimming around happily and healthily. She was ecstatic about the miraculous turnaround. When she asked the vet what was wrong, all he said was,

"He just needed some fish medicine," that's all.

How was the vet able to achieve this seemingly miraculous recovery in such a short period of time?

Puzzle #19 Final Destination for Bobby

Bobby had no parents. One day, his guardian decided that he could no longer afford to take care of him. So, the guardian decided to send him away to live in the country with relatives of his. Since the guardian had to work, he could not accompany Bobby on the train ride to the country. In addition, Bobby could not read nor write. So, the guardian placed a large label around Bobby's neck with Bobby's name and the address to where he was meant to go. Despite the fact that the railway staff was very helpful, Bobby never made it to his final destination.

Why didn't Bobby make it to his final destination?

Puzzle #20 Someone Had to Draw the Line

A research unit at a prestigious university wanted to test a group of people's perception skills. To this end, the researchers crafted a test in which they would evaluate their test subjects' skills. The test consisted of a single item that read this way:

Please observe the following image.

Now, please respond to the following question:
Can you determine which of the two lines is longer?

Puzzle #21 Swinging for the Fences

A farmer has a large field which is surrounded by a fence. In his field, the farmer has a barn with six horses inside. One night, the six horses were inside the barn. Then, lightning struck, and the sound of thunder spooked three of the horses. They busted through the barn door and ran outside. The other three horses stayed inside the safety of the barn.

Since the farmer was fast asleep after a long day of work, he didn't notice the lightning strike. In the morning, he went about his usual routine with all six horses.

How is this possible?

Puzzle #22 An Unusual Meal

A very large and crowded restaurant was bustling at lunchtime. It was a pleasant afternoon until Billy entered the restaurant. As soon as Billy entered, all of the customers in the restaurant left their meals, got up from their tables, and hurried out the door as soon as possible. No one even bothered to pay for their meals, much less ask for the check.

Why did the customers of this restaurant flee as soon as they saw Billy enter?

Puzzle #23 Where's the Dough?

An old miser walks into a bank. He walks up to the window and indicates to the teller that he is there to withdraw all the money from his account. The teller complies and gives the man all of the money in his account. The man then counts his money and asks the teller to deposit the money back into his account.

Why would the miser withdraw the money, count it, and then deposit it back into his account?

Puzzle #24 Going for a Ride

On one occasion, a married couple wanted to go on a vacation. When they went about booking their seat on the flight, the airline wanted to charge the wife extra, since she was so big and needed more than one seat. At the same time, the husband insisted that he shouldn't be charged the full fare for his seat, as he didn't take up the whole seat.

After some haggling back and forth, the airline agreed to charge the married couple for two regular seats even though the wife needed more than one and the husband didn't even take up the entire seat.

Why did the airline end up charging the married couple for just the two seats?

Puzzle #25 Paying the Price

A young college student walks to a counter. She talks to the man behind the counter and places a book on the counter. The man looks at the book and then tells the young lady,

"That will be five dollars, please."

The young lady places a five-dollar bill on the counter. The man takes it, and she begins to walk away. The young lady leaves the book on the counter. She does not go back for it, nor does the man call the young lady to come back for it. The young lady did not return to get the book at any time.

Why did the lady pay for the book but not take it with her?

Puzzle #26 Not Buying It

After a long day at work, Jimmy had dinner, and then decided to watch television. Around midnight, his local television station broadcast a weather update:

"The current rainstorm will continue for another two days. Please make sure to take the necessary precautions to ensure your safety. On the bright side, it will be warm and sunny in 72 hours."

Jimmy scoffed at the weather forecast and muttered:

"They got that one wrong yet again."

If the rain will continue for two more days, but then will become warm and sunny in 72 hours, how could the forecast be wrong?

Puzzle #27 Life is a Game

Henry is a young boy who wants to play video games all day and do nothing else. He doesn't want to go to school nor do his homework.

One day, Henry's father warned Henry that if he didn't get his act together, he would take away his video game console. Henry pleaded with his dad not to take away his console. Henry's father agreed that he could keep the console in his room, but if he didn't shape up, he would be unable to play with it anyway.

Sure enough, Henry didn't shape up. As per the promise, Henry's father left the console in Henry's room. He left the console intact, and he did not remove any of its components. Henry's father managed to solve the problem using a hammer and some good, old-fashioned elbow grease.

So, how is it possible that Henry's father left the console in his room, intact, but used a hammer to make it impossible for Henry to play with it?

Puzzle #28 I Dare You

Mike and Joe are drinking on a Saturday afternoon in Mike's apartment, which is 15 stories up. After some drinks, Joe's friend dares him to jump out of a window to prove he can do this without being injured.

Mike accepts the dare, proceeds to jump out of the window, and lands harmlessly on the street below.

How can Mike go through the dare without being hurt?

Puzzle #29 What Are You Up To?

Following a crime spree, where a man had been spotted shoplifting several times, the police decided to put up "wanted" posters all over the town. The police had been able to identify the man's face clearly as security cameras had captured his image. Witnesses had also identified the man seen in the security camera footage.

One day, two police officers saw this man. They were well aware that this man was a famous criminal. But, they did nothing to arrest him.

If the two police officers had seen this man who had been clearly identified as the robber, why didn't they do anything to arrest him?

Puzzle #30 It's Completely Puzzling...

A group of research students wanted to test the math skills of another group of students. The research students were looking to stump their counterparts to measure their ability to deal with complex issues. So, they devised the following exercise. Here are the instructions:

Please have a look at this number puzzle.

2	11	20
4	9	32

7	8	49
4	10	?

Now, please find the missing number. There is only *one* correct answer.

So, what do you think is the missing number?

Puzzle #31 Empty Space

Three men are walking together on the street. They enter into an empty building together, on foot, at the same time. After some time inside the building, the night watchman came in to find the building completely empty. The footage on the security cameras showed the men walking into the building, but not walking out.

What happened to the three men who entered the building when the watchman found the building to be completely empty?

Puzzle #32 Dude, I Can't Open the Door!

After a night of partying, a young man arrives home at his apartment. As he arrives at his front door, he finds that he is unable to open the door. Confused, he makes sure that he's got the right building. *Yes, he's got the right building.* Also, he makes sure that he's got the right apartment number on the right floor. *Check.* He was even greeted by one of his neighbors who offered to help.

This man struggled for a few more minutes before giving up. He sat down outside his door and passed out.

Why couldn't this man enter his apartment?

Puzzle #33 What a Pile Up

On a calm, sunny day, there were a large number of cars that crashed into each other. About 30 cars, trucks, and even buses were involved in the pile-up. There were even some military vehicles involved in the pile-up of cars. Most of the vehicles had been overturned. Some had been flung a long distance from the initial point of impact. Yet, no ambulances were at the scene, and no police arrived. No one was injured. There was no commotion and no reports in the news. Most importantly, no people were harmed as a result of this pile-up.

Why was the scene so calm despite the large pile-up of vehicles?

Puzzle #34 Whacky Weather

Joe was driving down the road on a bright, sunny day. Then, he came to a full stop and eased up slowly before it suddenly got dark. He had to roll up his windows as water began pouring all around his car. Next, the water stopped just as suddenly as it had begun. After that, a gust of wind enveloped the car. Finally, the sun came back out, and the man was able to continue his trip safely.

How are these sudden changes in condition possible?

Puzzle #35 Are You Lion to Me?

On a very warm Saturday afternoon, a woman was walking down a path. Suddenly, she spotted a roaring lion in the distance. The lion started running in her direction, yet the woman was unafraid and did not make any effort to flee. She seemed to be completely at ease upon the sight of the lion.

Why didn't the woman flee when she saw the roaring lion running in the distance?

Puzzle #36 A Letter to the Editor

A faithful reader of a local newspaper decided to write a letter to the editor, hoping to get her letter published in the Sunday edition of the paper. This is what she wrote:

Dear Editor,

Can you respond to the following question?

What can be found once in a minute, twice in a moment, but never found in a hundred years?

Sincerely,

Martha Smith

What do you think the editor's reply to this letter was?

Puzzle #37 The Hitchhiker's Tale

A hitchhiker is standing in the pouring rain. There are plenty of cars passing by, but no one stops to offer the man a ride. Finally, after quite some time in the rain, a car slowly passed by with its emergency lights flashing. As the car slows down further, the hitchhiker runs up to it, open up one of the car doors and jumps in. As he is clearing the rain from his eyes, he notices that there is no driver, yet the car is still moving. The hitchhiker begins to call out, but no one replies. Freaking out, he decides to open the door and jump out of the car. He lands safely on the street and runs away.

How is it possible for the car to be moving without anyone driving it?

Puzzle #38 Some Legalese for You

At a big law conference, the top lawyers in the country gathered for their annual meeting. The organizers decided to hold a contest to test the knowledge of the conference attendees. One of the questions posed during the contest was the following:

Did you know that there is one type of crime which is punishable by law if it is attempted, but is not punishable if actually committed? What crime are we talking about?

A very young lawyer immediately raised her hand and gave the correct answer.

What did she answer?

Puzzle #39 Mind your Ps and Qs

Here is a question that was part of a contest run by a local newspaper. The prize for the right answer was a free monthly subscription. Here is the question:

This particular word has 6 total letters. The 2nd, 4th, and 6th letters are the same. If you skip 7 letters, starting from the first letter, you get the 3rd letter. And if you skip 7 letters again, starting from the 3rd, then you get the 5th letter.

Can you determine what word we are talking about?

Puzzle #40 Tunnel Vision

Please look at the following image:

Now, here is the situation:

A truck wishing to enter this tunnel is one inch too high. Thus, it will get stuck if it attempts to make its way through the tunnel. There is no other way of reaching its destination aside from going through this tunnel. The driver must be at his destination in one hour, and has little time to spare.

What can the driver do to fit in the tunnel?

Puzzle #41 Now that You Mention It

Speaking of trucks, a police officer saw a truck driver going the wrong way on a one-way street. The street was clearly marked as one-way. But, the police officer said nothing to the driver and let him go on his way.

Why didn't the police officer do anything about the driver going the wrong way on a one-way street?

Puzzle #42 Color Me...

An old man decided to go live on his own in the wilderness. He wanted to get away from civilization to have the best possible view of the world. In the place he chose, he built a rectangular house, but given the location, he could only see south from any of the four corners of his new house. Then one day, he saw a bear pass by the front of his home.

What color was the bear that passed by?

Puzzle #43 Making the Grade

The teacher of a fifth-grade class was told that the school superintendent would be stopping by for inspection some time the following week. The teacher was very concerned about giving a good impression of both himself and the students.

The school principal told the teacher that the superintendent would be asking questions to the children, but that the teacher would be allowed to choose who responded to each question. So, the teacher needed to figure out a way where he could be sure that the student he picked knows the right answer.

The day before the superintendent arrived, the teacher gave his students some instructions where he could be certain that he would always pick a student who knew the right answer.

What instructions did the teacher give his students?

Puzzle #44 The Fly in the Coffee

In a busy coffee shop, a lady sat down to get a cup of coffee. The waiter served her a cup and a bagel. After a few moments, the lady called the waiter over and said,

"There's a fly in my coffee."

The waiter nodded and said,

"My apologies, ma'am. I'll get you another cup."

A few moments later, the waiter arrived with another cup of coffee. The lady had a sip and said to the waiter,

"Hey! This is the same cup as the one with a fly in it!"

How did the lady know she had been served the same cup of coffee but without the fly?

Puzzle #45 The All-Black

A man is standing in the middle of the road. He is wearing an all-black costume. His face is covered by a black ski mask. He is wearing black gloves. All the buildings in the town are painted black. The tarmac is all black, with no stripe painted on it. The streetlights are also painted black. Then, a totally black car, with black tint on its windows approaches the man. The car has its headlights turned off. Just as the car is about to hit the man, the car turned and avoided the man.

How was the driver of the car able to identify the man right before hitting him?

Puzzle #46 A Job Interview

A company is looking to fill a vacancy for a top-level executive position. The interviewer is talking to several candidates. The position calls for someone who is exceptionally sharp and perceptive.

The last candidate to be interviewed, a tall, young lady, is sitting in a chair at the end of the table in a large conference room. The interview sits at the other end of the table. The interview places a cup of warm tea before the young lady but without the tea bag inside of it and far away from her so that she wouldn't be able to get a glimpse of the drink without getting up. The interviewer then asks the candidate,

"What's before you?"

To this question, the young lady immediately replies, without getting up,

"Tea."

The interviewer smiled and offered her the job on the spot.

How did the interviewer know this was the candidate he wanted?

Puzzle #47 At Opposite Ends

In a business meeting, two colleagues are sitting at opposite ends of the table. There is no one else sitting at the table. But, they cannot see each other. There is nothing on the table either, and there is nothing else that could be obstructing their view.

How is it that the two colleagues cannot see each other despite the absence of obstructions?

Puzzle #48 Home Alone

Imagine that you are home alone at night. The power has gone out, and there are no lights. Your only means of illumination are a candle, an oil lamp, and firewood. Then, you realize that you only have one match to light up these items.

What do you light up first?

Puzzle #49 Happy Birthday

As part of the final examination in a philosophy course, the professor asked the students in her class to answer the following question:

How many birthdays can a person have throughout the course of their life?

Only one of the students got the right answer.

What did he say?

Puzzle #50 Drawing the Line

In an advanced math class, the professor posed this challenge to his students.

Please look at the following image:

In the middle of this box, there is a line.

Now, how is it possible to make this line shorter without erasing it?

Puzzle #51 Order in the Court

The following case was brought before a judge at the local courthouse:

There was a petition by a man to marry his widow's sister.

After carefully studying the petition and reviewing applicable legislation, the judge proceeded to deny the petition.

Why did the judge deny the petition?

Puzzle #52 Driving me Crazy

You are an Uber driver in your city. Today is a really busy day. First, you pick up three passengers at Green Street, and drop them off at Main Avenue. Then, you pick up one passenger at Blue Road, and take him to Second Avenue. Finally, you pick up two more passengers on Red Street, and take them to the Gold building back on Main Avenue.

Now, what is the color of the driver's eyes?

Puzzle #53 A Man and his Daughters

Jennifer's dad, who is a retired military man, has five daughters. His first daughter is Mary, who is blonde. His second daughter is Peggy, who is a brunette. His third daughter is Debbie, who is also a blonde. His fourth daughter is Susie, who happens to be a redhead.

So, what is Jennifer's dad's fifth daughter's name?

Puzzle #54 A Traffic Jam

A city with a terrible traffic problem has decided to do something about it, finally. The city mayor has decided to restrict the circulation of vehicles by limiting the number of cars based on their color. As such, blue cars can circulate on Mondays and Wednesdays. Red cars can circulate on Tuesdays and Thursdays. Yellow cars can only circulate on the weekends. Green cars can circulate on Fridays. None of the car colors previously indicated may circulate on a day other than the day in which they have been authorized.

However, you can drive your car for any day of the week.

So, what color is your car?

Puzzle #55 At the Mercy of the Court

A convicted felon has been sentenced to death. After throwing himself at the mercy of the Court, the judge has decided to give the convicted one last opportunity to pardon his life. If he chooses correctly, the court will spare his life, though not his conviction.

The court gives the man the option to choose one of three doors.

The first door contains a raging blaze that the man must get through.

The second door contains three lions that haven't eaten in four years.

The third door contains a firing squad that is ready to fire.

To save his life, the felon must surpass the obstacles behind each door.

Which door does he choose?

Puzzle #56 Oh My Son!

A man and his son were driving down a long, deserted road. Suddenly, a large truck came out of nowhere, and struck the car. The man who was driving was tragically killed in the accident. The son, who was the passenger, was rushed to the hospital in serious condition.

Upon entering the hospital, the son was rushed into the operating room for emergency surgery. The surgeon on call immediately recognized the son and said,

"I cannot operate on my own son!"

How is this situation possible?

Puzzle #57 Challenge Me!

A local radio station has decided to run a challenge. The radio host challenged listeners to name three consecutive days without using the following days: Tuesday, Wednesday, or Saturday.

The winner of the challenge would receive a gift certificate of $500.

After numerous attempts, the tenth caller got the right answer.

What were the three consecutive days that beat the challenge?

Puzzle #58 Out the Window

A window washer was going about his daily routine. He was cleaning the windows on the 35th floor of a large office building. Suddenly, he slipped and fell. He was wearing no safety harness, and had no other protective gear. There was nothing to slow his fall, nor to cushion his landing. He fell to the floor with no other injuries, aside from a bruised ego.

How is this possible?

Puzzle #59 Make Sure You Study for the Test

An English professor decided to make his students' final course examination simple. He gave his students a single sheet of paper with a single question. The ones who got it right would pass the course. Those who didn't would fail. The entire course was riding on a single question.

This is the question:

What word in the English language, when four of its five letters are taken away, maintains the same pronunciation?

The students had two hours to solve the answer.

There is only one such word in the English language. What is it?

Puzzle #60 A Cat's Meow

A pet shop ran a contest directed at cat owners. The winner would receive a free lifetime supply (the cat's lifetime) of cat food. After unsuccessful attempts by multiple participants, an 8-year-old girl figured out the right answer.

Here is the question:

Which side of a cat has the most hair?

It took the little girl less than a minute to give the answer.

What answer did she give?

Puzzle #61 Do What You Will

A man decided to have his will written up. In it, he stated that, while he was from Hawaii, he wanted to be buried in Texas.

When the lawyer read through his requests, the lawyer told the man that he could not be buried in Texas.

The will stated, "It is my will to be buried in Texas."

What reason did the lawyer give the man for not being able to be buried in Texas?

Congratulations on making it this far. You did a great job. You have certainly put in some hard work and brain power. Please remember that practice will help you get better in solving these types of puzzles. The more time you spend on these puzzles, the better you will become. In a way, it is just like going to the gym. But, with these exercises, you will be flexing your intellectual muscles!

Solutions to All Puzzles

In this section, you will find the solutions to each puzzle. Do take the time to go over each solution carefully. And, please remember, no cheating!

Puzzle #1 The Twins Dilemma
Solution: The twins' parents were relieved when they figured out that Rory was born on December 31st of one year at 11:59 pm, while Cory was born on January 1st of the next year at 12:01 am. Thus, they are identical twins and children of the same parents, but with completely different birthdays.

Puzzle #2 How Did the Farmer Cross the River?
Solution: The farmer must first take the sheep across, thereby leaving the wolf and the grain alone. Then, the farmer comes back for the wolf (or the grain) to take to the other side. Then, the farmer comes back across the river, but this time, he takes the sheep along. That way, he doesn't leave the sheep alone with the wolf (or the grain). Next, the farmer leaves the sheep alone and take the wolf (or the grain). He leaves the wolf alone with the grain on the other side of the river. The farmer then comes back for the sheep one last time. All three have now crossed the river successfully.

Puzzle #3 Mr. Jones' Math Class
Solution: If Mary speaks softer than Cindy but Josephine speaks more loudly than Cindy, then Mary speaks softer than Josephine. Hence, Mary will not be punished.

Puzzle #4 Speaking of Math Class...
Solution: The average score of the students who passed is 8. The average score of all 20 students is 6. So, 20 * 6 = 120. Next, the eight students that failed averaged 3. So, 8 * 3 = 24. After, subtracting the average score of those who failed from the class in total, 120 – 24 = 96. Finally, divide the remaining points among the number of students who passed (12). Thus, 96 / 12 = 8.

Puzzle #5 The Big Race in the City
Solution: The runners crossed the finish line as follows: B, C, D, A. The first runner to cross the finish line, and thus the

champion, is B. Then, C arrives next. So, B, C… then D is between A and C. Thus, the order is B, C, D, A.

Puzzle #6 Going on Vacation With the Bros

Solution: Alex is neither flying nor driving. Since Jack is with Alex, he won't be driving or flying either (we can assume any other means of transport such as a train). Andy is flying. Since Charlie isn't going with Mike, who doesn't fly, then Andy and Charlie are going together by plane. That leaves Tom and Mike, who are planning to drive. Hence, Tom is going by car.

Puzzle #7 A Family of Big Eaters

Solution: Ace and Buddy eat more than Scout. Buddy eats less than Precious. Precious eats more than Ace, who, in turn, eats more than Scout. So, Scout eats the least of all four. This means he won't be put up for adoption like the other three.

Puzzle #8 To Shoplift or Not to Shoplift?

Solution: The lady is an employee of the store. She filled the shopping cart with materials that were not items for sale, for example, trash, and proceeded to take it outside. That is why the store's security did not stop her.

Puzzle #9 A Bit Too Much Excitement

Solution: The man is in a movie theater, hence the dark room. He took a drink and began choking on an ice cube. After a few moments, the ice cube melts, and the man is able to breathe and speak again.

Puzzle #10 Tell Me What You See

Solution: The answer to the code for a free premium membership is: "Reading between the lines" as the letters of the word "reading" have been placed in between lines.

Puzzle #11 Which Way Is Up?

Solution: The man is very short. So, he can reach the button for the lobby very easily, but cannot reach the button for the 45th floor in the evenings. (It is possible for him to just wait for someone taller to get on and push the button for him, but why wait when you can take the stairs?)

Puzzle #12 Going Around in Circles

Solution: She works in a large office building that has a circular parking tower. Her parking space is on the sixth floor of the parking tower. So, she needs to drive in circles six times before reaching her spot.

Puzzle #13 That's All She Wrote
Solution: This lady is a business owner. She is signing her name on the weekly paycheck of her 60 employees. Hence, she must do this every week, because everyone is counting on their weekly paycheck.

Puzzle #14 Swing and a Miss
Solution: As the batter swung at strike three, the ball got away from the catcher. Since the catcher lost control of the ball, the batter ran down to the first base and made it there safely before the catcher got the ball. Hence, the batter struck out but reached first base on the passed ball by the catcher.

Puzzle #15 Burning the Candle at Both Ends
Solution: Rob works at night. So, he is up all night at his job. Then, he gets home in the morning and sleeps all day. This is why he isn't exhausted in the morning, even after not sleeping at night.

Puzzle #16 Child's Play
Solution: After combining their sand piles, both kids have one large pile of sand.

Puzzle#17 Your Wishes Are My Command
Solution: The servant made the following request to his master: "My mother wishes to see her grandchild playing on a pile of gold." With this wish, the servant was able to combine all three wishes into a single one.

Puzzle #18 Something's Fishy
Solution: The vet felt sorry for the sweet lady. He couldn't imagine how devastated she would be if her beloved fish died. So, he replaced her dying pet fish with an identical, healthy one so the lady wouldn't notice the difference.

Puzzle #19 Final Destination
Solution: Bobby was a dog. He had chewed through the name tag that was put on his neck. That is why the railway staff was unable to figure out where he needed to go.

Puzzle #20 Someone Had to Draw the Line
Solution: Naturally, line "B" is longer. By circling "A," an optical illusion is created by simulating that "A" has been chosen as the longer line of the two. This is meant to determine if the test subjects would use their own perception even though an incorrect answer was suggested.

Puzzle #21 Swinging for the fences

Solution: The three horses that escaped the barn did not go very far, because the fence kept them inside the farmer's field. The other three horses stayed in the barn. This is why the farmer was able to find the three horses outside of the barn, but within the fence.

Puzzle #22 An Unusual Meal

Solution: Billy was one of the animals that had escaped from the zoo earlier in the day.

Puzzle #23 Where's the Dough?

Solution: The miser wanted to make sure that the bank had all of his money on hand. (Depending on the amount, though, the bank may not have that much cash on hand and may have to order it).

Puzzle #24 Going for a Ride

Solution: Since the wife took up more than one seat, the airline billed her for one and a half seats. Since the husband didn't even take up the entire seat, the airline decided to bill him for half a seat. In total, the couple was billed for two seats.

Puzzle #25 Paying the Price

Solution: The young lady was paying the fine on an overdue library book, and did not check out any additional books.

Puzzle #26 Not Buying It

Solution: Since the forecast was broadcast around midnight, the broadcast was wrong, as it would be nighttime in 72 hours. Hence, it would be impossible for it to be warm and sunny.

Puzzle #27 Life is a Game

Solution: Henry's father used the hammer to build a shelf in his room so high up that Henry couldn't reach it even if he pulled up a chair. So, Henry's father let him keep the console, but he couldn't play with it.

Puzzle #28 I Dare You

Solution: Mike jumped out of a window on the first floor. Since the window is only 3 feet off the ground, Mike was able to land safely on the street below, thereby fulfilling the dare.

Puzzle #29 What Are You Up To?

Solution: The robber was already in jail. The two officers came into his cell to take him to court to face trial. Hence, they didn't have to arrest him because he was already in custody.

Puzzle #30 It's Completely Puzzling...
Solution: The answer is 36.
To complete this puzzle, you must multiply the first two numbers in each row and then subtract the first digit from the result of the multiplication so that you can get the third number in that particular row.
So,
$(2 * 11) - 2 = 20$
$(4 * 9) - 4 = 32$
$(7 * 8) - 7 = 49$
$(4 * 10) - 4 = 36$
Hence, 36 is the correct answer to the puzzle.

Puzzle #31 Empty Space
Solution: The three men had, in fact, left the building. They went into the building to get a car from the parking garage and then drove away. (Alternatively, the men could have left through another exit, but this is unlikely as the security cameras did not pick them up walking out.)

Puzzle #32 Dude, I Can't Open the Door!
Solution: Since the man had been partying and drinking, his friends decided to take his car keys away. His house keys were on the same key ring. His friends then got this man a cab and sent him home without his keys. Hence, he was unable to enter his apartment without his keys.

Puzzle #33 What a Pile Up
Solution: The vehicles were toys. A child had been playing with them and piled up them on top of each other as a part of his game. The child had even tossed some of them around.

Puzzle #34 Whacky Weather
Solution: The man drove through a car wash. First, it was sunny, then dark, then the water came, then the wind picked up, and finally, the sun came back as he exited the car wash.

Puzzle #35 Are You Lion to Me?
Solution: The woman was unafraid and made no effort to flee because she was at a zoo, and the lion was located securely in its pen.

Puzzle #36 A Letter to the Editor
Solution: Dear reader, Regarding your letter where you posted a question, here is my reply: The letter "M" can be found once in a

minute, twice in a moment but never in a hundred years. Best, the editor.

Puzzle #37 The Hitchhiker's Tale

Solution: The car was driverless because it had broken down. So, it was being pushed. The hitchhiker did not see the people pushing the car because of the heavy rain.

Puzzle #38 Some Legalese for You

Solution: Here is what the young lawyer said: Attempting suicide is punishable by law but cannot be punished if the individual takes their own life, as they are dead.

Puzzle #39 Mind your Ps and Qs

Solution: The correct answer is the word: DELETE. The 2nd, 4th, and 6th letters are "E." If you skip 7 letters starting from the first, you will get "L." Then, if you jump 7 letters again starting from the 3rd letter (L), you get "T."

Puzzle #40 Tunnel Vision

Solution: Since there is no other way around, and the height difference is only one inch, the driver has decided to deflate the tires just enough to fit under the top of the tunnel. Once through, the driver can then re-inflate the tires.

Puzzle #41 Now that You Mention It

Solution: The police officer did nothing about this situation because the truck driver was walking the wrong way on the one-way street. Hence, he was not breaking the law in any way.

Puzzle #42 Color me...

Solution: The bear was white. Since the man could only see south from all four corners of his home, he had to be atop the north pole. So, the only bears at the north pole are polar bears.

Puzzle #43 Making the Grade

Solution: The teacher instructed all of his students to raise their hands to answer every question. Those students who were sure they knew the right answer would raise their right hands. Those students who didn't know the answer would raise their left hand. Hence, the teacher would be certain which students knew the right answer and which ones didn't.

Puzzle #44 The Fly in the Coffee

Solution: Even though the waiter had apparently gotten a fresh cup of coffee, the lady knew that it was the same cup of coffee but without the fly in it because she had already put sugar in it.

Puzzle #45 The All-Black
Solution: Even though everything is painted black and the man was completely dressed in black, the driver was able to see him because it was broad daylight.

Puzzle #46 A Job Interview
Solution: Since the job called for an exceptionally sharp candidate, the interview was impressed to see that the lady had understood his wordplay: T comes before U, that is, P Q R S T... U... V W X...

Puzzle #47 At Opposite Ends
Solution: The two colleagues cannot see each other because they are sitting with their back to each other.

Puzzle #48 Home Alone
Solution: You must light up the match first before you can light up anything else.

Puzzle #49 Happy Birthday
Solution: Only one! As a person can only have the same birthday every year.

Puzzle #50 Drawing the Line
Solution: To make the line shorter, draw a longer line next to it. Such as this:

Puzzle #51 Order in the Court
Solution: The judge denied the petition because it is impossible for a man to marry his widow's sister as he is already dead.

Puzzle #52 Driving me Crazy
Solution: Since you are the driver, the color of the driver's eyes is your own eye color.

Puzzle #53 A Man and his Daughters
Solution: Jennifer's dad's first four daughters have already been named. So, Jennifer's dad's fifth daughter's name is Jennifer.

Puzzle #54 A Traffic Jam
Solution: As long as your car is any color that isn't blue, green, red, or yellow, you are free to circulate any day of the week.

Puzzle #55 At the Mercy of the Court
Solution: For the felon to save his life, he has to choose the second door, because the lions have already been starved to death after not eating for four years.

Puzzle #56 Oh My Son!
Solution: The surgeon about to perform the operation was the son's mother.

Puzzle #57 Challenge Me!
Solution: The caller named the following three consecutive days: Yesterday, today and tomorrow.

Puzzle #58 Out the Window
Solution: While the window washer was cleaning the windows on the 35th floor, he was cleaning the inside of windows. So, his fall only resulted in a bruised ego.

Puzzle #59 Make Sure You Study for the Test
Solution: The only word in the English language that maintains the same pronunciation even after four of its five letters have been removed is QUEUE.

Puzzle #60 A Cat's Meow
Solution: The side of a cat that has the most hair is the outside of the cat.

Puzzle #61 Do What You Will
Solution: The lawyer indicated that the man could not be buried in Texas because he was still alive. He needed to die first before he could be buried in Texas. Hence, the will would have to state something like, "Upon my passing, it is my will to be buried in Texas."

Now that you have seen the solutions to the puzzles, please don't spoil them! Give yourself a chance to work out each of the puzzles. Once you have reached an answer, then you can have a look at the solution.

Once you have seen the solution to a puzzle, try to see if there is another possible solution to the problem. The chances are that there is another possible solution to the problem without it being too wacky or too "out there."

Please keep the following concept in mind: The simplest answer is usually the right one.

So, take your time. Go through each item, and make sure you work out all of the possible solutions in your mind before you arrive at a conclusion.

Conclusion

Thanks again for purchasing this book. It was created with the intent to get your creative juices flowing and have some fun at the same time. Please take the time to go over each of these puzzles and figure out the best possible solutions for each one.

Once you have gone through each of the puzzles, you can lead your own sessions. You can get your friends, families, and colleagues to work on each of these puzzles while you lead the discussion. Your experience will certainly be useful in helping others get the most out of each one

In fact, it is always fun to speculate on alternative solutions. Often, you will find that thinking outside the box can lead to some wonderful discussion and debate. After all, creative thinking is all about finding alternate solutions to common, everyday situations. So, don't hold back. Do take the time to explore other possibilities.

If you liked this book, do check out the others in this series. You will find them to be just as fun and interesting. They will definitely provide you with hours of fun and entertainment.

As always, if you have found this book to be fun and interesting, don't forget to leave a comment. Other readers who are interested in picking up a book such as this will greatly appreciate your honest opinion. Hopefully, they will be able to get as much enjoyment out of this book as you have.

Thanks again.

See you next time!

Connect with us on our Facebook page
www.facebook.com/bluesourceandfriends and stay tuned to our
latest book promotions and free giveaways.

Printed in Great Britain
by Amazon

74986737R00071